Stone
by Stone

Stone
by Stone

Exploring Ancient Sites on the Canadian Plains

Liz Bryan

Heritage
House

Library and Archives Canada Cataloguing in Publication
Bryan, Liz
Stone by stone: exploring ancient sites on the Canadian plains /
Liz Bryan.
Includes bibliographical references and index.
ISBN 1-894384-90-3
1. Indians of North America—Prairie Provinces—Antiquities—
Guidebooks. 2. Prairie Provinces—Antiquities—Guidebooks. 3.
Stone—Prairie Provinces—Religious aspects. 4. Paleo-Indians—
Prairie Provinces. 5. Indians of North America—Prairie
Provinces—History. I. Title.
E78.P7B794 2005   971.2'01
C2005-901078-9

Heritage House acknowledges the financial support for our
publishing program from the Government of Canada through
the Book Publishing Industry Development Program (BPIDP),
Canada Council for the Arts, and the British Columbia
Arts Council.

Heritage House Publishing Company Ltd.
#108-17665-66A Avenue
Surrey, BC
Canada
V3S 2A7
greatbooks@heritagehouse.ca
www.heritagehouse.ca

Printed in Canada

To my son, David

Acknowledgements

A book such as this, which covers so much ground, both physically and intellectually, could not have been written without a great deal of help from experts in the field. I would like to thank the following for advice, information, and help with photos: Jack Brink, Provincial Museum of Alberta; John Brumley, in Havre, Montana; Richard Cherepak, John Dormaar, Lethbridge; Margaret Hanna, Royal Saskatchewan Museum; Tim Jones, Saskatchewan Archaeological Society, Saskatoon; Michael Klassen, Vancouver; Brian Kooyman, Calgary; Rod Vickers, Edmonton. Other people helped to make the fieldwork easier and more pleasurable. Among them are: Bonnie Moffet; Quenton Heavy Head; Dixie Green; Lorraine Goodstriker; Armand McArthur; Clifford Many Guns; Jeanette Many Guns; Ted and Allene Douglas; George and Margaret Tosh; Velma Booker; Doug Richards; Betty McFarlane; Tim Dutton; Tilley Duncan; David Munro; Michael Sherven; Kevin Hronek and the staff at the Minton municipal office. I thank you all.

Except where noted, all photographs were taken by Liz Bryan.

Contents

STONE,

the skeletal structure of Planet Earth, old and indestructible. If stone had a memory, what stories could it tell of fire and ice, upheaval and flood, of the very first creatures that crawled upon its belly? Stone anchors us to the history of the planet and of mankind, for we are not the first to have walked by it or on it, warmed it in our hands, found pleasure in its shape and colour, used it to make things from our imagination as complex as a cathedral and as simple as a tipi ring. Stone has energy; its magnetic field blends with solar winds to paint the polar skies. Stone endures, to tell us stories of the past, stories that echo the myths and legends—the oral history— of the first people to inhabit the plains, the hunters of the buffalo.

Stones from the Stone Age

The first European settlers to arrive on the prairies thought themselves lucky: there were no forests to clear. Instead, before they could begin to break the sod, there were stones, millions of them, littered across the landscape by Ice Age glaciers. Some boulders were far too big to move but others could be handled, hauled away in stone boats and thrown onto piles at the edges of the new fields. Thousands of hectares of grassland were thus laboriously cleared to make way for agriculture, though many of the farms, won so grudgingly from the tough prairie sod, failed in the harsh climate.

If settlers had looked carefully at the stones they moved off their fields, they might have seen that many were not just haphazard scatters but deliberate constructions by the people who came before them. The nomadic buffalo hunters used the land in a very different way, leaving traces of their vibrant civilization, both the spiritual and the mundane, in the very stones that the newcomers unwittingly shoved aside. In little more than a decade, the landscape that had sustained the first people for tens of thousands of years was, for the most part, permanently altered. Only those constructions that stood on land too isolated, too hummocky, or too finely dissected by creeks and coulees were saved. By the time historians and archaeologists

Zephyr Creek pictograph, adapted from Keyser and Klassen.

realized their significance, much had been lost in terms of material evidence, though testimony of another kind survived. The people whose ancestors inherited the grasslands and who continued to use them right up to the days of European infringement, are still here. And in their

Circles of stone scattered across the Bear Hills.

Ribstone at Herschel, Saskatchewan.
Both photographs by George Tosh.

myths and memories are stored the information we need to bring the archaeological evidence to life.

Stone configurations, lying on prairie grasslands where they were placed centuries ago, are hard and evocative evidence of the buffalo hunters' way of life, as alluring to today's traveller as any Old World monument, and many are just as ancient. Some arrangements of circles and cairns, known as medicine wheels, are older than Stonehenge or the Egyptian pyramids. Some of them reveal knowledge of the stars and perhaps reflect a search for deeper mysteries, a spiritual connection. Boulders were sometimes placed in recognizable shapes, often of men and turtles; others are the simple rings of campsites. There are also many buffalo jumps and eagle-trapping pits. More intriguing are vision quest sites and pictures painted or scratched on stone, signs of a spirit world still vital today. All are remnants of a lost way of life, a different history.

How many tipi rings in this rock pile?

Ancient sites like these can still be found on the short-grass plains. The search for them requires a journey not only through the lovely landscapes of southern Alberta and Saskatchewan, but into another time, a time so distant that only archaeologists can begin to uncover it. And only the memories of the First Nations peoples can bring it to life.

Ribstones at Viking, Alberta.

The Landscape

Opposite: Red Deer badlands, near Drumheller.

Prairie bedrock, born of thick layers of sediment accumulated over tens of millions of years, once lay submerged beneath a vast, shallow sea. In a fairly recent (in geologic terms) cataclysm, the Rocky Mountains to the west heaved skywards, buckled, and folded. Eroded rock and soil from the mountain upstarts were sluiced into the sea and gradually land emerged, a tropical land where giant beasts feasted and fought. But this was just the beginning, the raw canvas on which the picture of the prairie landscape was to emerge. The final painter was ice. In the past billion years, at least three great ice ages, each lasting 100,000 years or so, advanced and retreated. In the last, thick ice masses carrying huge rocks and debris from Hudson Bay to the north and the Rocky Mountains from the west, crept southward over the prairies, smoothing and smothering. For eons, hardly any land could be seen at all, only a thick ocean of ice. Then, around 12,000 years ago, the ice began to shrink.

Sandstone rocks at Writing-on-Stone.

Geologists can trace the most recent ice age by mapping terminal moraines, formed by the ice front's farthest advance, where humps and ridges of detritus and some mammoth boulders were abandoned as the ice melted. They can also point out where once gigantic ice dams created huge lakes and diverted rivers; and show what happened when these dams burst and water gouged escape channels—often 60 metres or more deep. Ironically, it was

Prairie fields of canola, near Herschel.

Fall migration in the southern Alberta foothills.

the furious gush of melting ice that bestowed such peaceful variety to the prairie grassland. It's a voluptuous landscape of hills and valleys and plains, of lakes and tiny twinkling potholes, of flower-filled coulees and vast sand dunes, its rivers flowing in deep valleys and canyons. In some of these, notably the Milk and the Red Deer, the canyon walls have been eroded by wind and water into fantastic badlands—caves and pinnacles, hoodoos and cliffs striped in many colours as different sediments are exposed. It is a

The Great Sand Hills, south of Sceptre, Saskatchewan.

Alberta badlands.

land where climate and soil conspired to create ideal conditions for a sea of grass where bison and other animals thrived and where the earliest inhabitants took nomadic possession, touched the land lightly, and left behind only modest signs of their passage. From the limestone peaks of the Livingstone Range, the great expanse of grass stretches east halfway through Manitoba, interrupted by the forested thrusts of the Porcupine and Cypress Hills; the badlands of the Milk, the Red Deer, and the Big Muddy; the sensuous curves of sagebrush uplands; and bony ridges of exposed sandstone bedrock. It is a magnificent landscape, a magnificent heritage.

Rocky Mountains from the Porcupine Hills.

One of the Coteau lakes, southeast of Minton, Saskatchewan.

Artifacts and Early Man

The meadows at Sibbald Creek where people camped 11,000 years ago and left behind a "stubby" Clovis point.

Stone spearpoints date from 9,000 years ago. Left: Alberta point; right: Scottsbluff.
Photograph by Bob Dawe, Provincial Museum of Alberta.

Found occasionally on the surface of the ground, but more useful to archaeologists if buried at levels where ancient feet in their moosehide moccasins once trod, are small stone implements, clues to the buffalo hunters' way of life. Made from many different types of rock, they provide a wealth of information—if one knows how to decipher the codes. From the sizes and shapes of the worked pieces archaeologists identify their function: household (chopper, knife, scraper) or hunt (projectile point). Because hunting was critical to survival, projectile points changed over the centuries as hunters honed their techniques and adopted new weaponry, and thus they provide a basis for scientific dating. When a radical change in shape or size occurred, it happened, seemingly, all at once throughout the grasslands, almost as if new people had moved in to displace the old. Occasionally this seems to have been so, though in some cases the changes indicate an advance in technology: from thrusting spear to hurling atlatl to the marvellous invention of the bow-and-arrow. But often the changes were simply stylistic ones; perhaps there were new fashions to follow.

The earliest stone points found in North America are large and leaf-shaped with a channel gouged out for a secure insertion of a bound-on shaft. These fluted points, known as Clovis and Folsom (all point styles are named for the site where they were first identified) were spear points and have

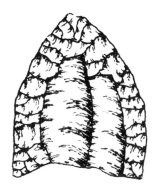

Bighorn sheep still come to Vermilion Lake for water. Their bones have been found in a 10,800-year-old campsite.

been dated at around 12,000 years old, some at kill sites of now-extinct Ice Age animals.

The bones of the people who made these fluted points have so far not been found in the southern prairies, but their weapons have, for stone endures. At Sibbald Creek, east of mountainous Canmore, Alberta, an 11,000-year-old campsite in a meadow between the aspens yielded sure proof of ancient man: little heaps of rock flakes and a beautiful green siltstone fluted point, of a variety known to archaeologists as "stubby," a short version of the Clovis

Short fluted point known as a Clovis "stubby."

point only found so far in Western Canada. The stone point had been made on the site: one of the flakes fitted back onto it perfectly. Farther west, at Vermilion Lakes, under the bony shoulder of Mount Rundle near Banff, an archaeological dig found traces of a circular shelter (a few post holes, a central fire pit, and clusters of stone artifacts and bone chips) that was dated at around 10,800 years ago, the oldest habitation found so far in Canada. While no fluted points were found, archaeologists believe, from the dates alone, that the people who sheltered here knew and used the technology.

Arctic willow at Vermilion Lake. First Nations people made painkilling tea from willow twigs. Willow has since been found to contain the main ingredient of aspirin.

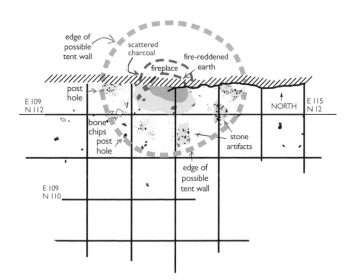

Plan of Canada's oldest habitation, more than 10,000 years old.
Courtesy of the
Provincial Museum of Alberta.

Opposite: Ancient horse blood was found on this Clovis spear point, picked up at the Wally's Beach site.

Giant footprints of long-extinct woolly mammoths on the dry bed of St. Mary's Reservoir.
Both photographs courtesy of Brian Kooyman, University of Calgary.

Wally's Beach Site

In southwest Alberta, where many of the rivers have been dammed for irrigation needs, water levels in the St. Mary's River reservoir northeast of Cardston had to be lowered for construction of a new spillway. As the water receded, the exposed surface of the lake bed was scorched by the heat of a prairie summer and several metres of dried surface sediments were whisked away by the steady Alberta winds. Revealed was a picture postcard from the

Pleistocene era of more than 11,000 years ago, an ancient mud floor, embedded with hundreds of tracks of Ice Age animals long extinct: woolly mammoths, camels (the only ones found in Canada), giant bison, and helmeted muskoxen. The tracks were so clear that experts could see where five camels had walked together and that one of the mammoths had a sore foot and walked with a limp. The St. Mary's River had once been a much-used watering hole—and a prime hunting site for ancient man.

Near the footprints, archaeologist Brian Kooyman and a team of researchers from the University of Calgary found telling conclusive evidence of man. Among the skeletal remains of several kinds of animals were the smashed vertebrae and butchered bones of a prehistoric horse, an animal that has been extinct for at least 10,000 years. Nearby were stone artifacts, including a chopper, scrapers, and

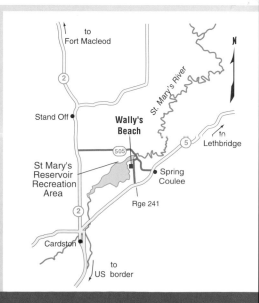

Brian Kooyman holds an 11,000-year-old Clovis point picked up beside Ice Age animal bones.

several well-formed Clovis spear points. These stone tools had definitely been used to kill and butcher. On them analysts found residues of ancient blood, which tested positive for musk-ox and horse proteins. Examination of the spear tips showed that they had been used to thrust into the animals. This is the first proof that early man in North America hunted horses for meat. (Ice Age horses were a different, smaller version of today's; when they became extinct, North America was without a horse until the Spaniards brought them over in the 1600s.) Carbon dating of the animal bones confirmed the age of the Clovis points and other artifacts as between 11,000 and 11,300 years. The material was a kind of chert that could only have come from quarries in today's Montana, some 400 kilometres distant.

"This site is one of the best preserved areas of ancient animal tracks in North America—possibly the world," says archaeologist Brian Kooyman. "It's providing us with an astonishingly detailed picture of what the New World was like during the late Pleistocene era." When the new spillway was complete, the St. Mary's River reservoir was filled up again, and the site is now under water, a condition that archaeologists hope will help preserve the incredibly rich—and incredibly ancient—hunting scene.

Researchers walk the dry lake bed at Wally's Beach.
Both photographs courtesy of Brian Kooyman, University of Calgary.

New Weapons

The Clovis point seems to have been the first stone point used by ancient North Americans, followed by the smaller and more finely wrought Folsom points, both used on thrusting spears. In the grasslands, the Clovis and Folsom points have been dated to between 10,000 and 12,000 years. Hunting techniques gradually changed and later, smaller projectile points, notched at the side for neater hafting, made their appearance. Archaeologists believe these were used on a revolutionary weapon, the spear-thrower or atlatl. Simple but effective, the device was a spear shaft hooked onto a second stick, which remained in the hand when the spear was thrown. The whip action increased both range and speed. Stone weights were sometimes attached to the throwing stick and these were often carved into animal shapes, perhaps to imbue the weapon with mystical power. Atlatls were used in Europe in the Paleolithic Era of 15,000 years ago, and how they made their sudden appearance in Canada is still a mystery.

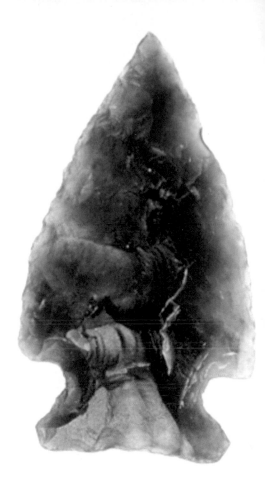

Side-notched stone point was the penetrating end of an atlatl projectile.
Courtesy of the Provincial Museum of Alberta.

Spears and atlatls continued to be the weapons of choice on the plains for the next 6,000 years, although their points were modified in size and shape over time. Then a brilliant invention, the bow-and-arrow, substantially changed the look of the stone points in archaeological findings. The new weapon seemingly arrived in Arctic Canada from the Old World about 4,000 years ago. During the next 1,500 years it gradually made its way south into British Columbia, then filtered east onto the prairies. By about 1,800 years ago, it was widespread in Alberta and Saskatchewan. Some archaeologists suggest that the bow-and-arrow made its appearance far earlier—perhaps as early as 8,000 years ago—and was used concurrently with

Stone atlatl weight.
Photograph courtesy of Tim Jones, Saskatchewan Archaeological Society.

Petroglyphs at Writing-on-Stone depict men with ancient weapons, including the multi-purpose bow-spear.

spears and atlatls. However old it is, there is no denying that the bow-and-arrow was a superior weapon for hunting and warfare. It offered both stealth and efficiency. Arrow shafts were smaller, easier to make, and lighter than long spear staffs. A well-sprung bow, probably reinforced with animal sinew, could deliver a powerful thrust, and from a great distance. Did this new weaponry indicate the influx of new people onto the plains? Some think so, because another innovation, clay pottery, made its appearance at around the same time. But it is also possible that only articles or ideas arrived, carried by people who commonly travelled far afield in order to trade.

The stone points needed to tip an arrow were smaller, lighter, and more delicately chiselled than spear points. The earliest arrowhead found on the Canadian grasslands, known as Avonlea, is obviously far too small for a thrusting spear. But how small would a point have to be to function as an arrow tip? Archaeologists have come up with an answer, based on the diameters of historic arrow-shafts: If the shoulder width of a projectile point measures less than 19 mm, it's an arrowhead; larger, it's a spear or dart point.

Tiny Toys

In some campsite excavations, arrowheads have been unearthed that are tinier by far than the norm, and imperfectly made. This had puzzled the experts, but recently archaeologist Bob Dawe has suggested that these were playthings, made for children's toy weapons, fitted to tiny shafts and used with tiny bows. And why not? Proficiency with the bow-and-arrow was vitally important to buffalo hunters, and the earlier boys mastered the skills the better. Toys are a good way for children to learn.

Avonlea

The Avonlea arrowhead signature point, dating from around AD 200, was first found during an archaeological dig near the Saskatchewan village of Avonlea. There are several interesting sites in the area: a large ceremonial circle, tipi rings, a buffalo jump, an unusual arrangement of 14 stone cairns on a single hilltop, and an effigy of a man, unlike any of the others (it's a small stick figure). The Avonlea and District Museum will provide guided tours to these sites, by prior arrangement. Call the museum: 306-868-2064.

Avonlea points.
Courtesy of the Heritage
Community Foundation

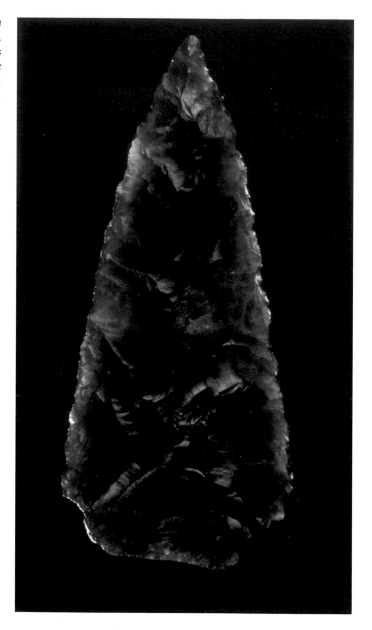

Knife River flint, from quarries in North Dakota, was sought out, perhaps as much for its translucent beauty as its utility.
George Tosh photograph.

Prehistoric Quarries

Whether for household tool or weapon, the type of stone used by the aboriginal inhabitants of the plains was critical: It had to be easy to chip and flake into the desired shape, yet also strong and able to keep a sharp edge. Utility was not the only criterion: Such things as colour, translucence, even the patterns in the stone, made the raw material more desirable. Was this because of a simple appreciation for beauty or a belief in the magic property of stone? The buffalo hunters travelled long distances in their quest for preferred material. When they found a dependable source,

The Rockies were no barrier to ancient peoples seeking good raw materials. Prehistoric quarries are found both east and west.

they visited it repeatedly over the centuries and carried home chunks for their own use, and for trade. At Yellowstone they found beautiful obsidian; at Knife River, North Dakota, hard, honey-coloured chalcedony; Mount Edziza in B.C. provided glossy volcanic obsidian; and at several different locations in southwestern Alberta, hard, multicoloured quartz or chert was found.

Analysis of the different types of rock can often pinpoint exactly which quarry they came from, and this helps clarify today's knowledge of ancient trade routes and travel patterns. At these prehistoric quarries, traces of mining activity can still be found. Men stripped away the surface soils, dug pits, pried rocks apart with tools of wood or bone—and left huge amounts of stone flakes and sometimes broken or imperfect tools.

Chert is a very hard rock that was used as early as 5,000 years ago by ancestors of today's Kutenai people from the west side of the Crowsnest Pass. It is found in a variety of colours, including black, though the Kutenai seemed to prefer coloured chert, perhaps believing it contained extra power or energy, and they were prepared to climb to great heights to obtain it. The rocks that make up the Livingstone Range in southwest Alberta are crusted over with gleaming white limestone, a material so white that even in summer the peaks seem dusted with snow. Underlying the limestone is a layer of chert which proved to be superior for tool-making. Prehistoric miners climbed onto the steep, high ridge overlooking the valley and dug down through the limestone, in places a metre deep, with their bone tools, antler wedges, and hammer stones. The richly coloured, unweathered rock, known as Etherington chert, was obviously worth the effort. Chert is hard as steel and chips readily into sharp flakes, making it ideal for weapons and tools.

Travel Info

The Livingstone Quarries sit high on a ridge near the Frank Slide Interpretive Centre in Alberta, their location marked by a power line tower. Here can be found the ancient quarry pits, depressions about a metre wide and half a metre deep, surrounded by a litter of chipped and broken rock. The view from the high ridge is stunning. Do not take away any of the rocks for souvenirs. The site is protected under the Heritage Act. The quarries are easily reached but be prepared for a fairly steep 2 km climb. Take the road that leads to the Frank Slide Centre, but keep straight ahead at the junction for a further 1.6 km. Park here and walk along a short stretch of four-wheel-drive track to a gas pipeline clearing; follow this uphill onto a track leading to the TransAlta tower on the saddle. Keep heading for the tower; you can't get lost.

Rather than transport large chunks of chert down the mountain, the men worked some of it into blanks, roughly cut tool shapes that could be chipped into final form later, or perhaps traded for other people to shape. The waste products of this manufacturing—piles of rock flakes known as detritus—still lie on top of the ridge. Archaeologists found huge quantities of fire-cracked rock at ancient campsites below, and they believe that here the Etherington chert was heat-treated to make it even harder and able to be sharpened to a long-lasting, fine cutting edge. Traded widely, items of heat-treated chert are found in many archaeological digs throughout the plains.

For nearly 2,000 years, rock from the Livingstone ridge quarries was the material of choice for plains people who hunted east of the Crowsnest Pass, and then, around 1,600 years ago, roughly the same time that the

bow-and-arrow came into use, the quarries were abandoned. There seems no good reason for this, except that perhaps other rock was considered more suitable for arrowheads. And different trade routes brought into the area beautiful flint from the Knife River quarries in North Dakota.

The Livingstone Quarries, high above the Crowsnest Pass.

Blood from Stone

Stone artifacts can be analyzed in many ways. Wear-use analysis on tool edges can reveal not only how the artifacts were used, but also what they were used on. Preserved fragments of plant and animal fibres on kitchen choppers give indications of diet, and DNA from ancient blood residues on knives or spear points can identify the different kinds of animal. It seems that each species of mammal, including man, has its own unique blood crystal form— so it is possible to tell whether bison, deer, antelope, or bear was on the menu. Sometimes even human blood is found; was it murder, or warfare? Blood is surprisingly durable, even over thousands of years. Techniques developed in crime laboratories enable it to be tested for antibodies that indicate prehistoric diseases. Its proteins can fix the date of death and can also be used in studies of genetics and evolution. All this information can be gleaned from a simple artifact, and yes, you can get blood from an ancient stone!

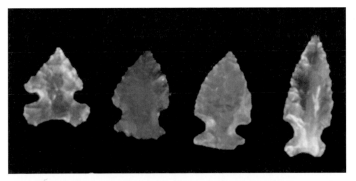

Projectile points from the bow-and-arrow period were made from many different coloured imported and local materials.
Photograph courtesy of the Provincial Museum of Alberta.

Pottery

It may seem odd to talk about ancient peoples by the names of their projectile point styles. After all, there probably were no Clovis people, or Avonlea tribe. But changes in spear and arrow points are the prime clues that archaeologists have to detect population changes, for exactly which early people inhabited the plains, and when, remains unknown. Populations, then as now, moved around quite a bit, and adopted new inventions, new designs, new fashions as they saw fit.

Assiniboine arrow points and pottery were found at the Lake Midden site, Saskatchewan. They are 400 years old.

However, in archaeological sites from later years (say, from 650 years ago), when most plains people had learned to make pottery, pottery styles become a major diagnostic tool, providing accurate dating: The amount of thermo-luminescence in the clay reveals when the pottery was first fired. And, as the prehistoric era approaches the historic, it also becomes easier to define tribal affiliations in various regions. Putting the two diagnostic artifacts, pottery and arrow points, together with what is known about tribal populations, archaeologists can be reasonably confident about ascribing artifacts to the ancestors of present First Nations people.

For probably the last thousand years, the ancestral Blackfoot people occupied much of southern Alberta; their pottery was made with thick walls and decorated with finger pinches, much like a pie-crust. Their arrowheads are side-notched, with straight or slightly concave bases. The Cree traditionally ranged in central Saskatchewan, though they moved readily in historic times. Their pottery is

Blackfoot arrow points and pottery were found at the Ross archaeological site, near Coaldale, Alberta. They are 500 years old.

known by its distinctive surface textures (mostly from being made within bags or nets) and adornments in the form of holes (called punctates) around the rim. Their arrowheads have narrow bases and rounded notches. The ancestors of today's Assiniboines lived mostly in southeastern Saskatchewan, and it is believed they might have originated south of the border, or at least be affiliated with more southerly tribes. Their fine, thin-walled pottery, with its distinctive sloped shoulders and intricate designs, matches the elegance of their arrowheads, which are straight-bottomed and finely notched.

Cree arrow points and pottery came from the Black Fox Island site, near Lac La Biche, Alberta. They are 450 years old.
All photos courtesy of the Provincial Museum of Alberta.

Buffalo and the Hunters

Opposite: Buffalo hide shield, Siksika.

How and when the first humans arrived in Canada is still open to debate. For many years, the firmly entrenched theory was that people followed giant beasts of prey across an ice bridge from Asia and down an ice-free corridor, east of the Rockies, to infiltrate all of the Americas. But today there are serious doubts about this corridor and whether people could have even survived on a bleak, ice-scoured landscape hedged in by retreating glaciers. Scientists now point to another scenario: travel down the West Coast, either by boat or across land that now lies under the ocean. (When the Ice Age held the world in its grip, seas were lower than today.) Geological studies in caves and undersea locations along the B.C. and Alaska coasts have found proof that habitable, ice-free land existed along the possible route as early as 14,000 years ago. The remains of bears found in caves on the Queen Charlottes, and stumps of pine trees dredged from under ocean waters substantiate this. Archaeologists are also beginning to find proof here of early human travellers: stone tools as old as 9,000 and 10,000 years.

Soapstone bison sculpture from Ardmore, Alberta.
Glenbow Archives C119-15.

The 2001 discovery of Ice Age mammals and early man at St. Mary's Reservoir in southern Alberta further disproves the ice-free corridor theory. Since the remains date from the time of maximum advance of the Laurentide Ice Sheet, people must have been already on the plains, feasting on muskox and horse meat, when the ice began its retreat, and must have arrived from a direction other than the ice-covered north.

We do know for sure that around 12,000 years ago, North American humans hunted and left their spear

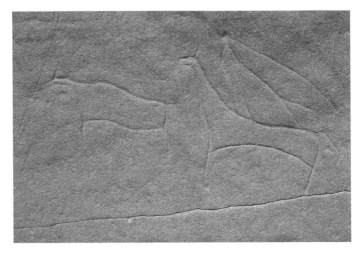

This buffalo chase, recorded at Writing-on-Stone, happened soon after horses were introduced. Notice the awkward position of the rider. Is he sitting sidesaddle?

points with the bones of huge Ice Age mammals. Then something happened to wipe these animals from the face of the earth, a sudden mass extinction that is generally blamed on Earth's collision with a giant meteorite. But there is also a suggestion that at least some of the animals, perhaps under stress from drastic changes in the environment, were hunted to extinction by man himself. Whatever the cause, the giant animals— mammoth, sloth, giant bison, muskox, and others— simply vanished from the fossil record. The horse disappeared along with them, but a smaller version of the bison (known colloquially as buffalo) survived to become the mainstay of the first grasslands civilization.

Most of the buffalo on today's plains are domesticated. Notice the ear tag.

The oldest bison kill site found so far in Alberta is south of Taber, near Chin Coulee. Here, 9,000 years ago, ancient hunters set up an ambush by a lake, hiding until the animals were close enough to spear. The strategy worked, over and over again. Here, archaeologists found piles of bison bones, spear points, side-scrapers, and other tools, all indications of successful hunting and of the meat and hide processing that followed.

Bison on the Plains

Bison found the ice-scoured plains east of the Rockies, covered with luxuriant grass, very much to their liking. Prairie grass is not only rich but also it retains its nutrient value even under the winter snows, and bison noses and hoofs are well adapted to scraping snow away. With year-round food and a climate steadily improving as Ice Age glaciers shrank, the American bison soon became the ascendant species on the grasslands. When the first European explorers came onto the plains in the eighteenth century, they were amazed: The huge, humped creatures (they called them, erroneously, buffalo, a name that persists) were so numerous that in places they blackened the land. Fur traders rode on horseback for days through great, unending herds. Pemmican (a kind of native power-bar made from dried buffalo meat mixed with lard and saskatoon berries) and buffalo jerky sustained the tribes throughout the winter as well as many a voyageur in his travels.

The buffalo of the plains (scientifically *Bison bison bison*) is huge, horned, and humped, and carries its thick, shaggy coat mostly on its front quarters. A big

Buffalo range near Waterton National Park, Alberta.

Native ceremonies often include the use of bison skulls, painted with tribal motifs.

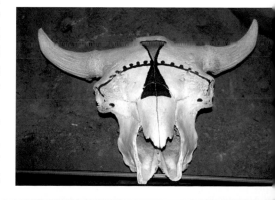

Plains people used buffalo hide for many things, including containers. Top: Envelope-style parfleche. Bottom: rawhide box. Photographed at Fort Carlton.

bull can weigh almost a ton yet run very fast—about 50 kilometres an hour. Subsisting entirely on the wiry short grass of the prairies, the vast herds were continually on the move. Buffalo live to an average of 20 years and are wily, suspicious creatures with a keen sense of smell but notoriously poor eyesight. Apart from man, their only predators on the ancient plains were wolves and the plains grizzly bear. Gregarious by nature (individuals seldom wandered away from the herd) buffalo were subject to mass stampedes, triggered by the slightest of reasons—or no apparent reason at all. This characteristic was put to good use by their human predators.

For thousands of years, the people of the plains relied on the buffalo; without them, it is doubtful if they could have survived, although we know they also ate deer, antelope, elk, small game, and even domestic dogs. And the buffalo provided more than food. From their shaggy hides the first people made covers for their tipis, shields, drums, clothing, and blankets. They used the bones for implements; hair for rope; sinews for thread; horns, bladders, paunches, and scrotum for containers; and dried dung (buffalo chips) for campfires. Buffalo chips were an indispensable commodity on the mostly treeless prairies. To keep close to their providers, tribes adopted a nomadic round, keeping track of the buffalo herds as they ranged seasonally in search of fresh grass and shelter.

The hunters of the prehistoric plains worked on foot, armed with spears, clubs, and bows-and-arrows, with dogs to help them haul their goods. It was only in the eighteenth century that they acquired horses from Spanish invaders in the south. Stolen or escaped from Spanish control, these animals, larger in size than the extinct native horses of North America, gradually travelled north to the Canadian plains. The Blackfoot called them "elk dogs." Horses and guns (obtained from fur traders in the north) changed hunting strategies entirely. It was far easier to hunt from horseback, and rifles were more efficient than bows-and-arrows, although the latter continued in use because they were cheaper and faster to reload than muskets. It was not long before the people of the plains were transformed from pedestrian hunters into probably one of the world's greatest equestrian societies. Horses not only revolutionized the hunt but changed other aspects of daily life. They could pull four times as much weight as a dog and for twice the distance, enabling the accumulation of more material possessions, including larger tipis. They could also haul greater loads of firewood and preserved foods, for more comfortable, and more sedentary, winter living.

Hide tipi and dog travois, at Wanuskewin, Saskatchewan.

There was a price to pay for this new mobility. Horses required much care and attention, particularly in winter. On the unfenced prairie, they strayed often and were easy to steal. They needed huge quantities of water, anywhere from 20 to 40 litres a day while they were grazing, and at least twice that much while hauling or running after buffalo. In summer, fresh grass supplied some of this liquid

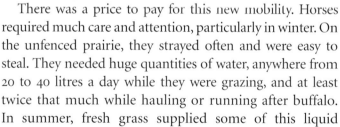

Horses revolutionized the plains way of life and are still very much a part of the prairie scene.

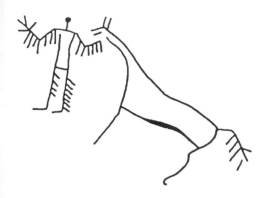

This figure, standing by his horse in his fringed jacket and leggings, might be a medicine man: Notice his long fingers. A petroglyph at Writing-on-Stone.

requirement, but the dry fodder of winter provided very little. The Blackfoot, who became masters of horse husbandry, watered their animals three times a day, even if it meant breaking the ice on frozen rivers.

Their new workhorses were also voracious eaters. To stay fit, they had to consume two percent of their body weight per day, which meant they had to be free to graze almost constantly for about 16 hours a day. Forage for horses in winter must have been a problem. They could paw their way through light snow, but in severe conditions, Blackfoot women had to clear areas of grass for them and provide supplementary food in the form of strips of cottonwood bark. The horses also needed shelter, for they froze easily. Archaeologists are finding signs that in order to accommodate the needs of their new acquisitions, the equestrians preferred to winter camp in sheltered, well-watered valleys.

One might find it odd that the equestrians of the plains still kept their packs of dogs, but dogs have some advantages over the horse. Being pack animals, they maintain allegiance to their human leaders and seldom stray. They need less than two litres of water a day, and in winter will happily eat snow. Food is easy—they eat meat scraps. Dogs rarely freeze, and they can be taken inside the tipi during extreme weather. In summer, however, because they cannot sweat, they overheat easily: All they want to do is lie and pant in the shade. Perhaps horses were more useful in summer and dogs in winter. In any case, as household pets, dogs were not lightly abandoned.

On horseback, hunters could range farther to find buffalo and many more could be killed on one hunt, often far more than were needed. When the supply of meat exceeded demand, only the tongues and the choicest portions were carried home, the rest being left to rot. But the hides of the slaughtered buffalo, useful for so many things and in high demand for trade, were always taken. First Nations people didn't know it then, but the advent of the horse meant the downfall of the buffalo. With the

influx of Metis buffalo hunters and hide merchants from the United States, the coming of the railway and the hunting of buffalo for sport, the immense herds dwindled and were soon all but gone. Of the estimated 125 million buffalo that once ran wild on the grasslands of America, fewer than 1,000 survived into the twentieth century.

One far-sighted hunter, from the Red River Valley in Manitoba, watched the swift decline, and in 1865 he captured some buffalo calves and kept them as a breeding herd. These animals were later sold and released into the wilds of Montana, but wild buffalo and the growing numbers of settlers on the U.S. plains could not easily coexist. The herd, then numbering 800, was bought by the Canadian government and released in Elk Island National Park, where they thrived. Some were later moved to Wood Buffalo National Park, where they interbred with the larger species, to Banff and Waterton National Parks, and to Wainwright, Alberta. A small group of animals that had escaped relocation made its own way into the Sturgeon River Valley, in the southwest corner of Prince Albert National Park, Saskatchewan. This herd, now numbering 300 to 400, is the only wild, free-ranging bison herd in Canada still within its historic range, and subject to the forces of natural selection, including predation and starvation. In 1972, four bulls and eight cows from Elk

There are many domestic herds of bison on the plains but most have been crossed with cattle. Only a few herds are wild and genetically pure.

Island were released into a paddock at Buffalo Pound Provincial Park near Moose Jaw. And in December 2003, 50 young buffalo (purebred Plains bison) were transported from Elk Island to Old Man on His Back Prairie and Heritage Conservation Area near Eastend in southwestern Saskatchewan. In 2005, bison are also being released along the Frenchman River in Grasslands National Park. The buffalo are gradually coming back where they belong.

Travel Info

At Buffalo Pound Provincial Park north of Moose Jaw, Saskatchewan, the natural topography of the sheltered Qu'Appelle Valley proved perfect for the construction of traps or pounds where aboriginal hunters stampeded buffalo into log corrals. Archaeologists have excavated sites here that yielded quantities of spear and arrow points, stone scrapers, and fragments of bone, evidence that the same pound was used more than once. It is fitting that a herd of buffalo has been re-established here.

The animals are fenced in a large area of open hillside where native mixed-grass prairie overlooks the waters of Buffalo Pound Lake. Visitors can climb onto a high viewing platform and walk along the Bison View Interpretive Trail (which is part of the Trans Canada Trail). Almost three kilometres long, it follows the paddock fence beside Nicolle Flats Marsh (where a boardwalk provides access for birders). Bison seek shade in the heat of midday. The best time to see them is early or late, or on cooler days when they might be walking the fence line down to their water supply. The park's trail brochure provides good information on buffalo, and provides a diary, explaining bison life throughout the year. The herd is fed with hay in fall and winter and kept healthy. Cows usually give birth every year, and an annual sale of calves prevents overcrowding. Bison can also be seen, if you are lucky, at Prince Albert National Park, at Old Man on His Back, and (soon) at Grasslands National Park, all in Saskatchewan.

Old Women's era spear or dart point.
Courtesy of the Provincial Museum of Alberta.

Thousands of buffalo rubbed this stone to a high gloss in Saskatchewan's Bear Hills.

Several rubbing stones were moved to a park on Signal Hill, in Estevan, Saskatchewan, along with replicas of tipi rings and medicine wheels.

Buffalo Rubbing Stones

Because buffalo shed their coats in summer, they are then vulnerable to brutal attack by insects, particularly on their hindquarters where the fur is thinnest. To counter the itching of mosquito and fly bites, they rub themselves on whatever is at hand. In the grasslands, the buffalo used large rocks left by the retreating glacial ice. Centuries of use have rubbed these rocks smooth, and centuries of stamping hooves have formed deep depressions or craters around these "buffalo rub" rocks. Run your hands over the surface and touch stone polished by thousands of itching buffalo.

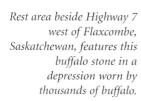

Buffalo rubbing stone on rangeland, north of Bow City, Alberta.

Rest area beside Highway 7 west of Flaxcombe, Saskatchewan, features this buffalo stone in a depression worn by thousands of buffalo.

Buffalo stone near Head-Smashed-In Buffalo Jump shelters horses in a nearby ranch yard.

Buffalo Jumps

Before the horse and the gun, during the thousands of years of buffalo plenty, plains hunters gradually developed increasingly sophisticated methods for killing game, methods that show unexpected organizational skills and suggest

a strong degree of social, even political, organization. One of the most successful—so successful it continued for thousands of years—was the buffalo jump. The topography of the grasslands, incised by steep river canyons and meltwater coulees, lent itself well to this strategy. In the fall, when the animals were fat, several tribes gathered to collect hundreds of animals and send them stampeding over high cliffs to their deaths. Then they divided the meat between families and preserved it for winter food. The drive was the focus but it could not begin until the proper ceremonies had taken place and the medicine men had found signs that the day was propitious.

Plan of bison effigy, still intact, near Big Beaver, Saskatchewan.

Sandstone cliffs at Head-Smashed In Buffalo Jump, Alberta. At the end of the escarpment, another jump known as Calderwood.

A communal buffalo jump was as carefully organized as a battle, the hunters divided into several regiments and playing different roles. Young men who were fast runners were trained as buffalo scouts and sent out to find the animals and bring them close. Above the cliffs, drive lanes, outlined by small heaps of stones covered with brush or buffalo dung, acted as funnels, narrowing towards the drop-off to keep the buffalo running in the right direction. Behind the piles of stones (known as "dead men"), a corps of men or women stood ready to jump into action if the buffalo went off course. Sometimes the scouts crept right among the herds, disguised in wolf skins or equipped with horn headdresses and rattles made of antelope hooves. They and the "dead men" along the drive lanes kept the buffalo moving steadily towards the cliff top, and then, when the animals could no longer veer away, the buffalo panicked and stampeded over the cliff. One benefit of a high cliff meant that most of the animals were killed, or at least badly crippled, easy targets for waiting bowmen.

The Blackfoot term for the slaughtering place was *pis'kun,* meaning deep blood kettle, an apt description of the aftermath: a heap of dead and wounded animals lying in their own blood at the foot of the cliff. Here, platoons of butchers took over command; live animals were quickly dispatched and the bodies cut up and hauled away to the nearby camp for processing. This was women's work. They skinned the animals, tanned the hides, and cut up the meat. Some was smoked and dried for pemmican. The bones were boiled to extract the marrow, but because the early people had no metal or even pottery containers, they scooped out a hollow in the earth, lined it with buffalo hide, filled it with water, and dropped in hot stones to bring the water to a boil. The stones were heated in open fires. Great concentrations of fire-reddened and cracked rock can be found today in any processing area excavation. Here, too, are the discarded bones of the slaughter, and often the stone implements used to kill and butcher. These enable archaeologists to tell when and for how long the jump was used.

Excavated bone-boiling pit at Head-Smashed-In. Courtesy of the Provincial Museum of Alberta.

Head-Smashed-In

Cliffs at Head-Smashed-In are made more colourful by lichen.

The largest, oldest, and best preserved buffalo jump on the Canadian prairies—and in North America—lies relatively intact on a high escarpment of the Porcupine Hills in southwestern Alberta. Though today the sandstone cliffs of Head-Smashed-In stand only eleven metres high, below lie bone beds another twelve metres deep, repositories of death that are probably 6,000 years old. The First Nations people were using this jump when European man was a primitive hunter-gatherer in the Neolithic forests, and they continued to use it sporadically (except for a thousand-year hiatus) until the middle of the nineteenth century. One estimate places the number of buffalo slaughtered here over the years at 123,000.

Enigmatic grooves above the jump. Are they tally marks or sharpening stones?

Assuming that the number of bison killed at a single time was 75, leading archaeologist Jack Brink has calculated that 15,000 kilograms of edible meat, fat, and organs were obtained after each jump. He estimates that in the processing area, southwest of the jump cliffs, there were more than 7,000 hearths and boiling pits and some ten million kilograms of fire-broken rock, 90 percent of it carried up from the valley of the Oldman River, several kilometres away. These figures suggest a huge surplus of meat, far more than even the largest tribe needed for winter supplies. Perhaps the processing camp was a kind of factory, which prepared buffalo meat and pemmican for trade to tribes outside the buffalo-rich plains or to European fur traders for whom it became a staple.

Head-Smashed-In is a World Heritage Site with an excellent interpretive centre and an unsurpassed location on the western edge of the plains. Its name is a translation from the local Piikani, whose legend explains it thus: About 150 years ago, a young man wanted to witness up close the sight of the buffalo tumbling over the cliffs. So he stood right under the sandstone lip as the animals poured like a waterfall down to their deaths. So many animals were killed that it took a long time for the carcasses to be moved. The young man was found among them, his skull crushed by the weight of bodies on top of him. They called the place *Estipah-Sikikini-Kots* or Head-Smashed-In.

Alberta's wooded Porcupine Hills catch some of the moisture that filters over the Livingstone range of the Rockies, and the prairie is also well watered by the tributaries of the Oldman River. In times past, the land provided excellent grazing for buffalo and the topography was just right for a buffalo jump. The sandstone cliffs of the escarpment were high enough and invisible from the huge reach of high grassland now known as Olsen Basin, where hunters knew they could find or bring buffalo. Here, even today, there are still hundreds of drive lane markers, small stone cairns covered with orange lichen, delineating three different sets

Crescent and cross, inscribed in the rock by the drive lanes. Is it the moon and the evening star?

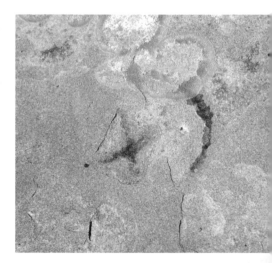

Bushes, including lots of roses, have grown up over the bone beds in the gully beneath the jump cliffs.

of lanes more than eight kilometres in length. On the high points that mark the edges of the main funnel, known as the South Pass, there are sandstone blocks, licked by the winds and incised with prehistoric petroglyphs. Did the watchers at the drive lanes sit here doodling with their flint knives? Or are the grooves and crosses and crescents ancient symbols of buffalo hunt magic?

The small terrace and ravine below the main jump are now bushy with shrubs and frequented by deer and marmots. It was here, back in the 1960s and 1970s, that archaeologists sliced down into deep layers of buffalo bones, each layer separated by soil that had blown over the bones in years when the jump was not used. They found deep deposits of soil without any bones at all. These sterile layers represent a known 1,000-year period of climate change known as the Altithermal when temperatures soared, drought conditions prevailed, and the buffalo moved north in search of better grass. The hunters, with their side-notched atlatl points, most likely went with them and the jump was abandoned. Wind-blown sand and soil gradually drifted over the bone beds, but when the climate ameliorated, other hunters, this time wielding bows-and-arrows, rediscovered the site and continued to use it for centuries more. Buffalo bones once again continued to pile up.

Archaeologists did more than excavate the bone beds: They went out onto the prairie, where, below the deep blood kettle of carnage, upwind from the reek of death and the flies, they found the campsites of the hunters and their families. Here lay signs of the activities that went on after the hunt: butchering, hide-tanning, the making of pemmican, bone-boiling, meat-smoking. The prairie flats must have been abuzz with activity. The work was hard and long. When all the meat had been processed and the prairie sky was pricked with stars, did the people gather around the campfires to feast and celebrate, give thanks, tell tales, sing songs, dance to the beat of buffalo drums?

In mid-summer, the Piikani hold their annual powwow at nearby Brocket. Hundreds of people gather, traditional tipis are put up, a pavilion is constructed using willow boughs from the river, the drummers sound off, and the dancing begins. Everyone dances, even the smallest children, and all wear traditional costumes, bright colours, and feathers. Smoke rises from open campfires; there are buffalo burgers and Indian fry bread; the sky darkens, and as the stars glitter, still the drumming and the dancing continue. It's a spectacle not to be missed.

Powwows bring out all the traditional finery for the dance.

Many First Nations people still use their tipis in summer and at traditional gatherings.

The Piikani used to hold their powwow at Head-Smashed-In. The Canadian Blackfoot Nation is composed of the Siksika or Blackfoot, Piikani or Peigan, and the Kainai or Blood tribes. According to their history, their lands used to stretch over much of southern Saskatchewan and Alberta.

Travel Info

At Head-Smashed-In, after careful archaeological testing of the proposed construction sites, a visitor interpretive centre was built, an intriguing, multi-level design that mimics the buffalo jump itself. Tours start at the top, and work down. Constructed inside the cliffs, west of the main jump, the centre brings to life not only the activities of the jump, but the lives and legends of the buffalo hunters, complete with voices from the past. It is also very much a focus for the local Piikani who guide the tours, staff the facility's gift shop and cafeteria (buffalo stew, fry bread, and bannock are on the menu), and participate in displays of dancing and drumming (every Wednesday afternoon in the summer). The Sunday learning series (February to May) features interpretive hikes and craft workshops, including making moccasins and traditional Blackfoot beading.

Across the road from the centre, on a high bluff overlooking the line of willows that marks the Oldman River below, the Piikani have set up several tipis where tourists can stay overnight. At $125 per tipi per night it sounds like expensive camping, even with shower facilities at the museum, until you realize that each of the large, round tents can accommodate 6 to 10 people. Also offered are one- and two-night cultural immersion packages, which include food at the cafeteria, guided

hikes (sometimes to the drive lanes), lessons in tipi-raising and other native arts and practices, and Piikani legends round the campfire. Starry nights and sunrise at this tipi camp are well worth the price of a sleepover. For a schedule of events or to book a tipi stay, phone: 403-553-2731 or email: info@head-smashed-in.com Web site: www.head-smashed-in.com

Head-Smashed-In Buffalo Jump lies 18 kilometres northwest of Fort Macleod, Alberta, along Springpoint Road (Secondary Road 785) reached from Highways 2 or 3.

The park offers intriguing badlands (watch out for cactus attack) and sheltering trees by the Red Deer River.

Dry Island

The farthest north of any known buffalo jump is at Dry Island, beside the Red Deer River, now a provincial park. This is one of Alberta's scenically splendid places, a great sweep of eroded badlands that displays some 80 million years of earth history—including the time of the dinosaurs—in its deep canyon carved by glacial floodwaters about 200 metres below prairie level. The river, today only a shred of its former size, swirls swiftly through stands of cottonwood and rosebushes around a large meander, a cut-off "dry island" of untamed prairie, sheltered from the prairie winds above. Here, archaeologists have found, beneath cliffs 50 metres high (the highest of any known jump), thick layers of buffalo bones and a few stone points that revealed the site's great age of 4,000 years. The jump continued in use, off and on, until about 300 years ago.

The park has no interpretive centre and none is needed. The area is wild and beautiful, perhaps just as the ancient hunters knew it; the river swirling through the willows is a favourite with canoeists and fishermen. In late July and August one can witness a curious phenomenon: goldeye fish surfacing in huge numbers to feed on clouds of newly hatched mayflies. Watch this at dusk, with a flashlight.

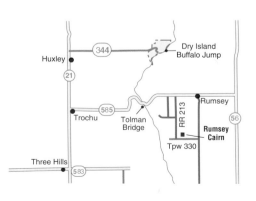

Travel Info

Dry Island Buffalo Jump Provincial Park lies on an isolated part of the Red Deer River's west bank. Take Highway 21 north from Trochu and turn east just past Huxley along Township Road 344 for 19 km. The road is rough and unpaved as it winds down to the canyon floor and is unsuitable for long trailers. (Park at the top of the hill, where there is a superb viewpoint.) The park is for day use only, but just before you reach the park, the Buffalo Jump Canyon Ranch provides camping and horseback guided trail rides. www.buffalojumpcanyon.com.

Old Women's

In the Alberta foothills, just a little north of Head-Smashed-In, sandstone rocks at the edge of Squaw Coulee near Cayley mark the site of another a buffalo jump. It was revealed when a flash flood in 1952 exposed a sheet of white bones. Archaeologists were quick to move in. They uncovered bone beds seven metres deep and were able to distinguish 29 different cultural layers, the bottom ones containing spear and atlatl points, the top layers with arrowheads. The change in technology appeared to take place about 1,400 years ago, a bit earlier than archaeologists had expected.

This site, known as Old Women's Buffalo Jump, is doubly interesting because it features prominently in local native legend, a version of the Adam and Eve story, with a twist. It goes like this, as related by a member of the Blackfoot tribe to Glenbow archivist Hugh Dempsey:

"In the early days of the world the men and the women used to travel in different camps. The men had their chief; the women had theirs. One day Napi (a trickster deity, known as the creator of things) called the men together and said: 'Why should we live apart from the women? If we all live together, then we can spend our time hunting and going to war while the women can do the cooking and tanning of hides.'

Prairie buffalo beans. When they were in bloom, buffalo were in rut and the hunters stayed home. The grasslands provide good birding and spectacular sunsets. This is an American goldfinch.

The buffalo jump, across Squaw Coulee.

"The men thought this was a good idea so Napi went in search of the women. He found them near the foothills, where they all lived in a large camp. Nearby they had a large buffalo jump, which was their main source of food. This was the Women's Buffalo Jump near Cayley. Napi met the leader of the women and told her the plan. The woman chief agreed and asked Napi to bring the men to her camp so that each woman could choose a man to be her partner. Napi returned to the men and told them the news. He had noticed many beautiful women at the camp and made plans to get the best one for himself. He stole from the camp and, dressing himself in women's clothes, he went to the women's camp and decided which one was the most beautiful.

"Before he had time to return to the men, they arrived and the women began to choose their partners. The woman of Napi's choice saw a man she liked but Napi intercepted her and told her to choose him. The woman, however, wanted the other man and bypassed Napi in favour of him.

"Napi then went to the next most beautiful woman and the same thing happened. Finally, when all the choosing had been done, Napi was the only one without a woman. In anger, he went to the buffalo jump and changed himself into a pine tree. And there he stood, alone, for many, many years."

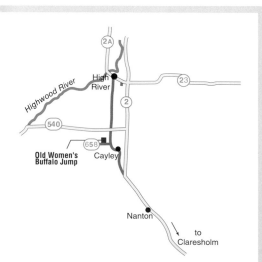

Travel Info

Old Women's Buffalo Jump lies along road 658 northwest of Cayley, a small village north of Nanton. It's a pretty spot; the eroded sandstone bluffs are photogenic, and in spring the yellow flowers known as buffalo beans grow in the coulee. The bone beds and excavations have been covered up and the lone pine tree, petrified Napi, is no longer to be seen.

Gull Lake

In Saskatchewan, the best-known buffalo jump site is on an escarpment of the Missouri Coteau near Gull Lake. Here, people who used Avonlea arrowheads rounded up bison and drove them over a shale bedrock cliff into a pound at the bottom of a steep coulee. Archaeologists uncovered here six distinct layers of bones, the earliest dating from around 1,800 years ago. Each bone layer was separated by a thick layer of earth that had slumped from the cliff above. From the two metres of deposits, 133 arrowheads were recovered. It seemed that only a few of the animals were killed by the fall, and the rest had to be killed with bows-and-arrows. It also seemed as if the owners of the arrowheads didn't care to retrieve them. Were those elegantly crafted stone points worth so little? Or was it considered unlucky to use an arrowhead more than once? These are the questions that archaeologists cannot answer.

The drop at Gull Lake doesn't seem very deep, but it was very successful as a buffalo jump.

Travel Info

The town of Gull Lake lies about equidistant from the Cypress Hills and the Great Sand Hills. The jump itself is southwest of the town. While nothing remains of the dig, the site is interesting, a great curving cliff top dropping to a now bushy coulee below. The jump is on private land, but if you want to visit, contact rancher Tim Dutton.

Roan Mare

Roan Mare buffalo jump overlooks a wide coulee. The escarpment ends in a tower of eroded rocks.

In southern Saskatchewan, where an old glacial spillway known as Big Muddy has gouged a deep, wrinkled scar into virgin short-grass prairie, a red rock escarpment some 12 metres high drops down above a steep talus slope into Roan Mare Coulee. Before archaeologists knew of the place, it was a haunt of outlaws who came here with their bands of stolen horses. A roan mare was left in the coulee to lead stolen horses across Big Muddy Lake, back when Big Muddy really lived up to its name.

Under the cliffs, archaeologists uncovered several bison kill sites and two separate sets of drive lanes extending more than five kilometres east through the prairie above. The drive lanes are marked with an estimated 7,000 small clumps of rock set 2.5 metres apart. Smaller kill sites have been identified on the west side of the valley, along with more drive lanes, a large number (1,627) of tipi rings, possible sweat-lodge

The coulee in summer is awash with yellow mustard.

locations, and other rock arrangements. The spectacular jump rocks, the drive lanes above (beware of cactus), and the beauty of the coulee—its floor in summer awash with yellow mustard—make this buffalo jump well worth a visit. There is an excellent interpretive sign.

Travel Info

Take the well gravelled grid road which leaves Highway 6 at the southern edge of the town of Minton and follow it west around several bends until you come to a road north signposted for a home, which can be seen down the hill. Follow this road; it will drop steeply down to Roan Mare Coulee and the jump site.

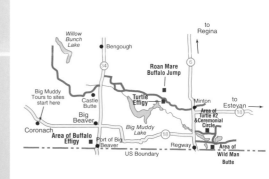

This glyphstone, with a buffalo face, was found near Trochu, Alberta.
Glenbow C254-5.

Buffalo Effigies

Buffalo gave life to the people of the plains, and were understandably revered. Small, natural stones that resemble the heavy shoulders and hump of a buffalo are known to the Blackfoot people as *iniskim* and are kept in medicine pouches, along with other sacred objects. They were used during ceremonies to call the buffalo. Most of these stones are pieces of fossilized ammonite or bivalve from the Upper Cretaceous fossil-bearing shales that are exposed in river valleys of southern Alberta.

When Canadien Jean L'Heureux lived with the Piikani in the mid-1800s he visited a tributary of the Red Deer River, where he was shown animal bones extruding from the cliff. "The enormous vertebrae measure up to 20 inches in circumference," he wrote. "The natives say that the grandfather of the buffalo is buried here." These were undoubtedly the fossilized bones of a dinosaur.

There are several legends attached to iniskim but the most widespread tells of a young woman who, when the hunters in her family had not found game for a long time, left on her own to find food. She heard singing in a nearby coulee and followed the sound, but there was no one there, only a strange stone singing a strange and wonderful song. The stone said that if the woman learned the song and kept the stone safe in a buffalo hide pouch it would always call the buffalo close so that her people would not starve. The woman took the stone home where others in her camp also learned the song. And from then on, the iniskim, kept safe in a medicine bag, was always called out to bring in the buffalo.

Iniskim, or buffalo lucky charms. The top one is a natural fossilized bone; the one below, a replica made of soft stone.
Courtesy of Tim Jones, Saskatchewan Archaeological Society.

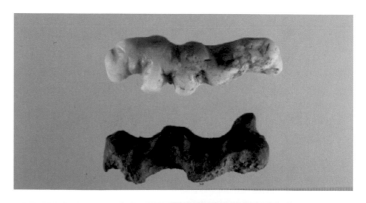

Ribstones

Some buffalo effigies are much bigger than iniskim, far too big to be portable. The grasslands are scattered with boulders left by the retreating glaciers of the Ice Age, and a few of these, in strategic positions on hilltops where hunters could watch for approaching herds, were carved into buffalo shapes and inscribed with magic signs. Known as ribstones, the three-dimensional sculptures are generally done on light-coloured quartzite millions of years old that originated on the Canadian Shield. Perhaps these rocks were selected because they were mysterious, markedly different from the run-of-the-mill prairie stones. Laboriously, using only tools of stone or bone, the first peoples carved these lumps of rock to depict the backbone and ribcages of buffalo, and added lines of small, deep circular pits known as cupules, or little cups. As works of art, the ribstones are powerful pieces and they are still objects of veneration.

Ribstones near Viking, Alberta, are still on their original site.

Two-part ribstone from Endiang is now in the Reynolds Museum at Wetaskiwin, Alberta.
Glenbow Archives, C208-2.

Viking

Ribstones in winter.
George Tosh photograph.

Ribstones still on their original site can be seen southeast of Viking, Alberta. There are two of them, part of a rock cairn on top of a small but sharp hill at the edge of the plains. The smaller has been carved down both sides into parallel ridges (ribs) with the backbone running down the centre; the larger stone, also carved with ribs, seems to be lying on its side. Both are light-coloured, almost white, and both are pockmarked with cupules. Despite the cultivated fields below and the highway close by, there is a sense of mystery about the place. When I was there, on a fine fall day with the wind restless and the clouds scudding, I found that two small braids of sweetgrass had been left as offerings on the ribstones and several pieces of coloured fabric danced in the shadows in a clump of poplars behind the hill. The First Nations people of the area still come to this sacred place, and echoes of their reverence linger.

Sweetgrass braids left as an offering.

Travel Info

The ribstones, designated as a heritage site, are a short drive from Highway 14, south of Viking. Marked by a large descriptive sign on the highway, the stones are on private land, surrounded by a short fence. There is a small parking lot. Treat the site with respect. It is unattended.

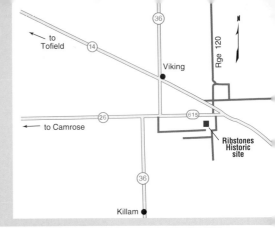

Coloured fabric streamers hung from nearby trees show that the ribstones still play a part in local native culture.

Sleeping Buffalo

This carved granite ribstone is extraordinarily similar to the ones at Viking, but is more than 600 km south, near Malta, Montana. Originally on a hill, overlooking the U.S. section of the Milk River, it has been given horns, eyes, nose, mouth, and even a tail.
James Marshall photograph.

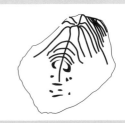

Herschel

In Saskatchewan, there is at least one fine ribstone, plus two smaller stones, possibly related, in a beautiful setting above Coal Mine Ravine southwest of the village of Herschel. At first glance, the flat-faced rock here is not at all similar to the rounded, buffalo-hump boulders of Viking. But there is a backbone and there are ribs. And lots of round cupules. The ribstone here seems to represent a one-dimensional buffalo, or a buffalo killed and splayed flat. Experts categorize the art style as Pit and Groove, the oldest form of rock art in North America, and they recognize stylistic similarities between the ribstone here and those at Viking.

The largest of the Herschel stones, known locally as Henry's Rock, is a slab of pale dolomite, a kind of limestone, with a flat, triangular face protruding a good 1.5 metres from the ground. Bisecting the triangle is a carved backbone, with ribs on either side, and the enigmatic cupules are arranged in rows between the ribs. Near the top of the boulder are two bisected circles that seem like eyes but could also represent bison hoofs. The designs wrap around the sides of the monolith, and on the top there is a curious coiled design, a bit, I thought, like a bison's tail. A short distance south lies a second, smaller stone where the buffalo representation (if it is one) seems more enigmatic: just straight parallel lines, two or three

curved ones, and a dozen cupules. These two are within sight of each other. A third stone, just a tip sticking out of a bank, lies a distance away. A fourth stone was once found, but before it could be examined, it had been scooped up and buried in a local farmer's stone pile.

Excavations around the edges of Henry's Rock revealed that the ribstone design continues another 50 cm below ground and includes another pair of "eyes," this time just circles, imprinted with three cupules. Radiocarbon dates from animal bones recovered from the dig suggest the carvings are at least 1,500 years old. Many ancient offerings from several eras were found, including projectile points, ritually broken pottery, glass beads, and a brass bracelet.

Archaeologists think that the three Herschel stones might have formed part of a ceremonial complex. Certainly, the setting above Coal Mine Ravine is one of the most extraordinary and beautiful on the grasslands. Aboriginal hunters have been coming to the sheltered and well-watered valley for more than 5,000 years to hunt and to collect berries, and perhaps to gather at the ribstone. The hilly terrain, broken by sandstone outcrops, has never been cultivated, and the untouched prairie is ablaze in early summer with wildflowers. Bushes along the folds and edges of the coulee provided berries for native pemmican, and in fall their flaunting colours transform the valley. Buffalo bones can still be seen eroding from the banks of the creek where excavations in 1996 uncovered a jump with two metres of bones plus fire pits and artifacts some 2,000 years old.

Nearby sandstone deposits, once the floor of an ancient sea, have yielded fossils of great age: two giant marine plesiosaurs, clams and snails that date back 65 million years, and a nautiloid that is even older, probably 500 million years old. There is also history of a more recent vintage. Winding through the area are tracks of Red River carts which once creaked along the old Carlton Trail. In the 1930s the coulee was mined for coal (hence its name) though little trace of industrial activity remains.

Two other modified stones at Herschel are less generously marked; only a few grooves and cupules suggest they belong to the ribstone complex. In summer, the hillsides carry huge mats of cactus.

Henry's Rock, its striking design emphasized by snow.
Photograph by George Tosh.

Ancient Echoes

The ribstone complex and other native sites, including tipi rings, a turtle effigy, and a buffalo rubbing stone, are looked after by Ancient Echoes Interpretive Centre (open 10 a.m. to 5 p.m.) with headquarters in the old Herschel School. Guided tours to the sites of this magical coulee take place three times a day, all year round. Longer hikes can be arranged by calling in advance. In addition, special events such as wildflower tours, native craft demonstrations, and full moon hikes are held in summer when a tearoom is open to provide refreshments. Phone: 306-377-2045 or e-mail ancientechoes@sasktel.net The Web site is interesting: www.ancientechoes.ca

For more of the First Nations experience, you can attend the Rainbow Culture/Survival Summer Camp in a tipi village at Coal Mine Ravine. A co-operative venture with the Battlefords Indian and Metis Friendship Centre, it aims to share with new Canadians aboriginal world views, legends, and life skills. Guests will prepare smoked buffalo meat, make pemmican, learn the art of primitive fire-making, pipe ceremonies, and natural medicines, and discover how to put up a tipi. If tipis are not being used for a camp, they rent out at $50 a night: Each tipi sleeps eight. Contact Ancient Echoes for information.

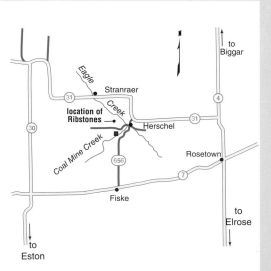

Travel Info

The village of Herschel lies northeast of Rosetown, Saskatchewan. Take Highway 4 north for 11 km, go west on Highway 31 for 23 km, then dip south on Secondary 656.

Ringing Rocks and Cupules

Were the cupules found on ribstones and other rock art on the grasslands used to make musical sounds? It is a serious proposition. Some rocks have a natural percussive quality: When struck they produce sounds similar to a bell or a drum and of varying resonance, depending on how hard they are hit. Repeated and carefully aimed blows with a hammer stone would produce both sound and rhythm—and leave round indentations, exactly like the cupules on stones known throughout the world as "ringing rocks." These were thought to produce special musical effects for ancient ceremonies. Could the ribstones at such places as Viking and Herschel have been used

for similar instrumental accompaniments? Apparently hammering into the rock cupules would imitate the sound of thundering hoofs—a kind of magic to draw the buffalo close. For more on the subject of acoustic archaeology, read *Stone Age Soundtracks* by Paul Devereux, published by Vega (2001).

The cupules on the Herschel ribstone might once have been used to mimic the sounds of the drums in buffalo-calling ceremonies. Drumming is still very much a part of First Nations tradition. These are drummers at the Siksika Fair.

Ancient Architecture

Opposite: Siksika tipi, photographed at the August powwow.

For tens of thousands of years, the people of the plains made their homes in buffalo-hide tents or lodges anchored by rings of stones, a form of housing so perfect for their way of life that there was no reason for it to change. One of its advantages was portability: it was easy to dismantle and transport. The tipi (sometimes spelled teepee) is conical, an ideal form of shelter for a nomadic people living on windy grasslands in harsh winters and hot summers. Supported by a framework of pine poles, the cone is slightly tilted, steeper at the back for strength and wind resistance, with a large circular or oval footprint and tapering walls. More than tall enough to stand up in, it is easily heated in winter by means of a small central fire. An opening at the apex lets out the smoke, and the vent has two flaps attached to outside poles which angle to catch the wind or keep it out it in bad weather. Around the inside of the tipi, a lining, about two metres high, adds insulation and prevents condensation.

Sunset over the Rockies: reflected light and shadows project ghostly images of tipis.

In summer, the height of the tipi keeps the interior cool, and natural air-conditioning can be induced by rolling up sections of the perimeter cover. Well anchored to the ground, usually with a central interior guyline and, in the past, by a ring of prairie stones (though sometimes by bone or wooden tent pegs), it is architecture so well suited to its environment that it has remained the same for thousands of years. Only the material has changed: Today heavy canvas has replaced the traditional buffalo-hide covers.

Tipi Designs

Above: One of the best places to see tipis, in all their different colours and designs, is at a First Nations powwow. These were at the Siksika Fair held near Blackfoot Crossing, Alberta

Opposite page: Tipi poles were traditionally jackpine. Even today, we call the trees Lodgepole pines.

Opposite page below: Otter design tipis of the Piikani.

To the people who called them home, tipis or lodges were sacred spaces, circular like the earth and with tall poles that linked them to the spirits who lived in the sky. Tipi doorways always faced east, so that in the morning, when the door was opened, the people could send their prayers to the rising sun. An easterly orientation also faced the tipi away from the prevailing west wind. The wooden pins that fastened the doorway covers were often hung with rattles made from the hoofs of the sacred buffalo.

The tipis of past eras varied in size, from 2.5 metres to 9 metres in diameter, with a mean of 4.5 metres. The average tipi would have used 12 hides, a large medicine lodge as many as 22. The hides of the cow buffalo, being thinner, were preferred. It took about 10 days to tan each hide, using

The word "tipi" comes from two words in the Sioux language meaning "used to dwell in."

Where wooden tent pegs were used, they had to be made of black birch. In Blackfoot legend, a strong wind tried its best to blow Napi off his feet and he was saved only by hanging on to a black birch tree. This bent under the wind, but did not break. Even today, birch tent pegs are preferred as anchors.

lye from alkaline lakes, buffalo brains and liver, grease, and soaproot, and longer to cut and stitch the tipi cover, which was usually made in two pieces for easy transport. Women made the covers and were responsible for setting the tipis up and taking them down, as well as for their transport, and the tipi belonged to the woman who made it.

The five-metre-long, straight wooden tent poles, usually of pine from the Cypress and Sweetgrass hills or the Alberta foothills, were considered family valuables—five good lodgepoles could be traded for one horse. But, wherever they went, the people had little trouble finding stones to anchor their tipis. What a sight it must have been: the band, on foot, slogging across the prairies carrying huge burdens and

Smoke from the central fire spiralled out through the smoke hole at the top of the tipi. The flap could be closed in bad weather.

Siksika Star tipi at Banff.

accompanied by as many as 40 pack dogs hauling sleds known later as travois. These were A-frames made from poles linked near the middle, to make a carrying basket to hold tipi covers, robes, and other goods—even small children. The routes they commonly took, between known good camping and hunting country, or to tribal meetings, can in some places still be found, because the travois poles left deep ruts in the prairie earth.

When Europeans appeared on the plains with their trade goods, the natives were quick to realize the advantages of canvas for tipi covers. Canvas was easier to work, much lighter to carry, and could more easily be decorated with totemic emblems.

Legend of the Buffalo Tipi

Some of the tipis near Head-Smashed-In Buffalo Jump in southern Alberta bear the imprint of two buffalo and a small red dog. The design commemorates a Piikani legend, a legend that is doubly fascinating because it seeks to explain the thousand-year gap that often appears in the archaeological deposits. Scientists attribute this hiatus to the Altithermal, a time in the Earth's cycle when the southern grasslands became too hot and dry, and the buffalo moved north.

The legend, in brief, features Napi or Old Man, the trickster god of the Siksika. When the buffalo disappeared from the prairie, the people prayed to Napi to help them. He set off, along with the son of a chief, to find the buffalo and bring them back. He searched for a long time, and one day, when he saw a single tipi by a stream, he became suspicious because no one ever camped by themselves, away from the tribe. To get close, Napi changed himself into a dog and the chief's son into a digging stick. The people in the tipi had a small son who saw the dog and took him home, along with the digging stick. Napi noticed the man go out and bring home buffalo meat. Next morning, the woman took the digging stick in search of roots and Napi the dog followed her. Near a cave, they spotted a buffalo cow; Napi ran into the cave, and the stick followed. Inside they found a whole herd of buffalo and other game, and they drove them all out. Once again the prairie was full of buffalo, and Napi and the chief's son led them towards their home camp, where the people eventually feasted.

On the Head-Smashed-In tipi the story is told in pictures. On either side of the doorway are two racing black bison, male and female. Notice the two spots on the backs of the animals, representing the kidneys, and the single spot above the eyes, which is the brain. The arrows coming into their mouths are spirit lines, which end at the heart. The cave in the story, and the little red dog, are painted directly behind the entrance. Around the peak of the tipi, against the black of the night sky, are the stars of the Milky Way; near the ground, the yellow grass of the prairie is spangled with fallen stars.

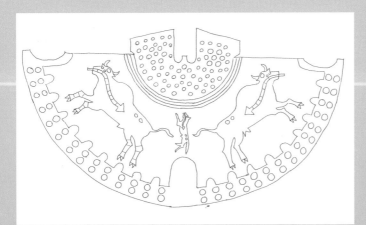

The tipis have different designs, different stories. But the female animals are always portrayed on the south side (which corresponds with the area inside the tipi allotted to women and their tasks), male animals on the north. Animals usually have a lifeline running from the mouth to the heart. Each piece of the design has meaning. For instance, a cross is said to be a butterfly or moth—a dream being which brings messages. The upper part of the tipi always represents the sky, with circles for stars; seven circles portray the Big Dipper; six, the Pleiades. Around the base of the tipi, the designs nearest the ground are representations of earth: rounded bumps for foothills, points for

Cree tipi at Wood Mountain, Saskatchewan. Below: The Saamis tipi and one of the story boards.

mountains. Each tipi design was traditionally given to its owner in a dream, and acts as a conduit between the owner and the spirit animal portrayed on it. The right to use a design is handed down within the family and can be transferred only during a special ceremony.

The biggest tipi in the world, originally built for the Calgary 1988 Winter Olympic Games as a symbol of Canada's native heritage, stands as a tourist attraction beside the Trans-Canada Highway east of Medicine Hat. Built of steel and concrete, it reaches 20 storeys high, weighs almost 1,000 tons, and can withstand winds of 150 kilometres an hour. This is the Saamis Tipi, its open-air walls decorated with ten round storyboards depicting

aspects of native life. It was erected at this site for a very good reason. Below the huge construction, in Seven Persons Coulee, lies an excavated ancient campsite where buffalo were killed and processed. Projectile points, ceramic sherds, and lots of animal bone were found here, including that of bison, wolf, deer, and antelope.

Where to See Tipis

In Alberta, there are always many tipis at the Calgary Stampede and at the tribal powwows; one of the biggest of these is the Siksika, held on the reserve southwest of Gleichen, where a huge new dance arbor is itself in the form of a tipi. There's also a Siksika Star tipi at their interpretive centre in Banff. (The Siksika claim an area around Castle Mountain as their traditional ground for collecting medicinal herbs and pine saplings for their tipi poles.)

Clockwise, from top: Tipis at the Siksika Fair, Alberta; Wanuskewin, Saskatchewan; Fort Carlton, Saskatchewan; Head-Smashed-In Buffalo Jump, Alberta.

In Saskatchewan, tipis can be seen at Fort Carlton National Park, Wood Mountain, and Wanuskewin, and at any of the tribal powwows. Camping in authentic tipis, usually including some cultural immersion experiences, can be arranged at Wanuskewin, north of Saskatoon (www.wanuskewin.com); at Piapot Plains Cree First Nation Village northeast of Regina; at Herschel (306-377-2045); Head-Smashed-In, Alberta (403-553-2731); and at several other locations.

The Tipi Liners

The wall of the Livingstone Range—a veritable picket fence of shining white limestone—rises sharply above the plains west of Alberta's Porcupine Hills. To the Blackfoot, these mountains, marking the edge of their traditional territory, were known as the Tipi Liners because they looked like the strip of hide or canvas that was hung around the inside of the tipi for extra warmth. The Livingstones (Tipi Liners) were also used to predict the weather. Changing atmospheric conditions make these mountains appear near or distant. When they seem close, it is going to be cold.

Tipi Rings

Tipis, the traditional dwellings of the plains people for thousands of years, left their circular footprints all over the grasslands of Alberta and Saskatchewan. The stones used to anchor them to the earth still remain in high, uncultivated places, the commonest by far of all the stone relics of buffalo days. Circles of fist-sized and larger rocks, they were used to hold down the covers of the nomads' tipis in their temporary encampments. Since each ring or encampment of rings was used only once, it is little wonder that there are still so many. One estimate places a million rings or more still standing on the Alberta plains! And there must be at least another million in Saskatchewan.

Many of the prehistoric campsites were on high land where lookouts could easily spot herds of approaching buffalo or enemies, or where the prairie wind could lessen the miseries of wetland mosquitoes and flies. When settlers arrived, some of the land preferred for tipi sites was either too dry or too broken up for agriculture,

Tipi rings above the South Saskatchewan River, near Medicine Hat, have been dusted with flour for easier mapping and photography.

and this is why so many rings remain. Some are almost buried by centuries of wind-blown soils; others are still vividly prominent in the prairie grass, simple yet moving evidence of everyday habitation. Here people lived for a while, warmed themselves by the fire, ate and slept, comforted their children, dreamed and loved and mourned and kept alive the legends of their tribe. Then they moved on, to set up house all over again.

To date, the oldest tipi rings found in Alberta date from the Oxbow period, 4,000 to 5,000 years ago. Archaeologists can tell much from these simple stone constructions: A double ring might indicate the use of stones on both the inner liner and the outer skin of the tipi, indicating winter habitation, a sign further reinforced by the presence of an interior hearth. Circles of small, widely spaced rocks or rocks in clusters would be evidence of summer use, when the tipi need be only lightly anchored or even rolled up to allow ventilation. If one side of the circle has heavier rocks, this might show the direction of the prevailing wind.

For most of their time on the plains, the buffalo hunters had only domesticated dogs to help them haul their homes and their goods from campsite to campsite. From the diameter of each stone circle left on the plains, archaeologists can calculate the length of the poles needed and the number of buffalo hides required for the cover. An average-sized tipi cover in the "dog days" would weigh

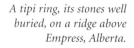

A tipi ring, its stones well buried, on a ridge above Empress, Alberta.

about 185 kilograms, and since each animal could pull only about 25 kilograms in a travois, seven or eight dogs would be needed to haul just one. When the tribes acquired horses, which could haul far greater loads, the sizes of tipis and tipi rings in general increased.

Tipi rings found in contemporaneous clusters on the grasslands usually number between three and four. Allowing seven people per tipi, one can infer that each camp numbered between 25 and 30 people. Basic arithmetic will show that they would have needed at least 30 dogs just to transport the tipi covers, let alone the rest of the baggage. And 30 dogs would eat as much as 100 kilograms of meat, or the equivalent of the proceeds of half a buffalo, each day. No wonder they needed so much buffalo meat!

At times, family groups met and camped together, perhaps for a communal hunt or ceremony. Where this took place, sometimes scores of tipi rings are found, often arranged in either a circle or a semicircle. At the British Block Cairn (see "Medicine Wheels"), some 20 to 30 tipi rings are arranged in a giant horseshoe open to the north. It is assumed that these were all occupied at the same time, implying a great gathering of perhaps 200 people. How did they know where and when to come? And what ceremonies or tribal negotiations might have taken place here?

Aerial view of tipi rings, arranged in a giant horse-shoe, next to the British Block Cairn north of Medicine Hat, Alberta. John Brumley photograph.

Where to See Tipi Rings

Grasslands

Flowing through Grasslands National Park in Saskatchewan, the Frenchman River provides the only dependable year-round water between the Saskatchewan River to the north and the Milk River to the south. On this beautiful land, the largest tract of virgin prairie left in Canada, archaeological surveys found more than 3,000 First Nations sites. The park's hills and coulees provided prime spring and summer hunting grounds for Gros Ventres, Assiniboine, Blackfoot, and Cree, and they left many traces here, of buffalo jumps and pounds, of medicine wheels and effigies—and of tens of thousands of tipi rings.

A good introduction to the park is the Frenchman River Valley Ecotour, a 28-kilometre auto-tour that highlights stops of interest, including a fine example of a buffalo rubbing stone with tipi rings nearby. More rings are to be seen along the Two Trees Interpretive Trail, which follows

the edge of the river for 1.5 kilometres. And there are others, now among the burrows of a prairie dog town, along the 15-kilometre North Gillespie Trail. Like other remnants of the pre-contact past, these stones must not be disturbed.

Lemsford Ferry

Near Lemsford Ferry, one of several that cross the South Saskatchewan River in Saskatchewan, 125 tipi rings have been counted on a bench above the river. As a protected site, this area can only be visited with a qualified guide. Contact the Saskatchewan Archaeological Society for assistance (www.saskarchaeological-society.ca). The site lies 20 kilometres north of the village of Lemsford. There is a regional park on the south side of the river.

Saskatchewan Landing

Saskatchewan Landing Provincial Park, beside Lake Diefenbaker, displays two areas of tipi rings. Its three-kilometre "Rings, Ruts, and Remnants" trail leads high above the lake, passing an old Metis homestead and pioneer trails, to a spectacular view, some well-defined tipi rings, and a buffalo rubbing stone. Good signage. Other rings lie to the west, along Smart Trail. Call in at the Goodwin House Visitor Centre for a map.

Carmangay

The nine tipi rings above the coils of the Little Bow River near the village of Carmangay, Alberta are easier to see when the grass is short but they are mapped and interpreted in a fine little picnic area beside Highway 23. It's well worth a stop if only to admire the river meanders. Excavations at the rings found only a few broken stone tools, some stone chips, and a few scraps of buffalo bone. But a small triangular  projectile point gave a rough date: anywhere from AD 200 to 1700. In the Carmangay municipal campsite, you can sleep in a tipi for a small fee.

Medicine Wheels

Dark Horse medicine wheel on the Suffield Reserve near Medicine Hat. The stones have been dusted with flour for study purposes.

The medicine wheels of the North American plains have been compared to Stonehenge, and they are as old, or older. But unlike the English construction, whose giant stones were quarried from afar, medicine wheels were built of the relatively small stones that the last Ice Age left so liberally on the grasslands. These stones were not worked but merely laid down in patterns on the prairie sod, humble constructions that can lie almost unnoticed on the landscape, particularly if the grass is high after good spring rains. Of all the ancient stone configurations found in Canada, they are perhaps the most enigmatic. No one as yet knows for certain what they represent, although archaeologists agree that at least some were holy sites, places of prayer and power, perhaps related to the Sun Dance, the greatest of the plains ceremonies. They have also been interpreted as death lodges, astronomical observatories, summer solstice calendars, boundary markers, and navigational aids. They provoke much speculation.

While the word "medicine" is appropriate (it is used by the Blackfoot to denote the mysteries of the spirit) the word "wheel" is not. Of the more than 70 medicine wheels so far discovered, only a few look anything like a traditional spoked wheel, though all have some circular component and some have radiating lines and central cairns or hubs. No two are alike. While they have been studied by geologists, astronomers, and mathematicians, most of the research has been archaeological, part of the painstaking

No wonder medicine wheel designs were in the round. There are circles everywhere, in the sky and on the ground. Even flowers seem to grow in round clumps.

uncovering of prehistory that is still on-going. Because of their great age and enigmatic nature, these special sites will always be mysterious. They are sacred places of great power, and their special auras cannot be denied. If you visit one, you will know what I mean.

I remember once searching for a medicine wheel north of Brooks, Alberta. It was late, and I raced not only the coming darkness but a thunderstorm that was drifting my way like a black jellyfish. I thought I was in the right place but I couldn't find the wheel. The prairie grass was high and sibilant; the wind roared and tore at my shirt; the first fat drops of rain came stinging down. I turned to leave: There was always tomorrow. But the sun slid miraculously out through a crack in the dark sky, and suddenly, all around, the stones of the wheel revealed themselves, glowing in a fierce electric brilliance. Magically, I was right in the centre of a ring. As the storm raged, I felt for a moment as if I stood in the vortex of the universe, a conduit for all its ancient power. I remained rooted to the spot, while the wind and the rain continued their attack,

as thunder boomed and lightning speared down. It was a mystical experience that I shall never forget. I am sure the hunters of the plains experienced such feelings.

Medicine wheels, all of them remote and situated on high promontories, are considered sacred to the First Nations peoples who often leave offerings—a twist of tobacco, a bundle of sage, or a tumble of coloured prayer flags. While the lines and circles might seem meaningless today, they were constructed with a definite purpose in mind, even if that purpose has been forgotten. The placement of the stones is important, and should never be tampered with. No stones should ever be removed. Visit such sites with respect: Some of them are ancient temples; all are irreplaceable testaments to the human spirit.

Aerial view of Roy Rivers medicine wheel above Empress, Alberta.
George Tosh photograph.

British Block Cairn, with many stones in the deep grass.

Archaeology

British Block

In 1965, archaeologists from Alberta's Glenbow Foundation excavated the British Block Cairn, a large medicine wheel on top of a hill known as The Lookout in Suffield Military Reserve north of Medicine Hat. This 26,000-hectare reserve (once known as the British Block because it was land reserved for settlers from Britain) has been closed to the public for almost a century, and most of its land has never been settled or ploughed. Still used for military exercises and partly protected as a wildlife preserve, the out-of-bounds area contains many traces of the ancient prairie peoples. So far, 2,000 sites have been found, most of them stone circles and cairns.

The British Block cairn is huge, almost nine metres in diameter and about 2.5 metres high, a pile of lichen-encrusted stones that, from far away, can be seen as a definite blip on the horizon. While the prairie surface nearby is well-endowed with stones, most of them still seem to be in place. The cairn must have been built, stone by stone, from boulders carried onto the hilltop, a time-consuming exercise. A 26-metre-diameter circle around the cairn has been partly disrupted: Early cowboys rearranged some of

Aerial photograph of British Block Cairn.
Glenbow B167-A-77.

the stones to spell out their initials or local cattle brands, and a figure of a man inside the giant circle has been somewhat disturbed. But it is still an awesome, imposing place, with far-reaching views south and east across the prairie.

When archaeologists excavate such a site, they usually leave at least half undisturbed, for further research. Half of the British Block Cairn was stripped down in layers, stone by stone, in the expectation of finding some clues as to when and why it was built. But the artifacts found were jumbled and out of sequence, of several different styles and therefore time periods, some as old as 5,000 years, others as young as 500, a conundrum that can only be explained if the artifacts were offerings, the older ones being prized possessions, perhaps kept by a family for generations. Pieces of pottery, a very late plains addition, were scattered throughout. No human remains were found, but there were bones from several different species of animals. The study results suggested that the cairn was not added to over the years (like cairns on mountain paths) but built all at once, probably around 500 years ago, the age of the youngest artifact. Around the medicine wheel, a huge number of tipi-rings—representing enough lodges to house perhaps 200 people—were arranged in a giant horseshoe, open to the north. Important ceremonies must surely have taken place on this high hill. Protected within the Suffield Military Reserve, this splendid piece of ancient architecture cannot be visited, except with an archaeologist and by prior permission.

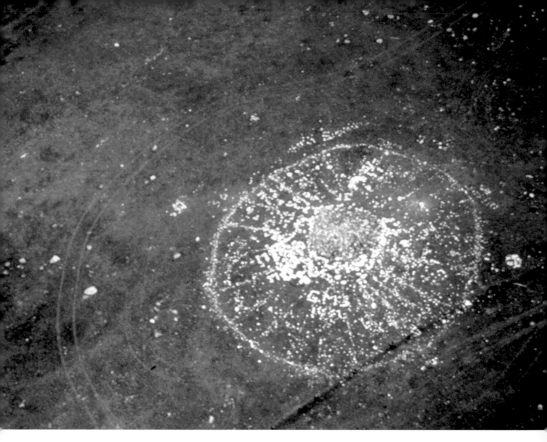

Majorville

The Majorville Cairn and medicine wheel sits on a small but sharp hill overlooking the Bow River (nearer to Bow City than to the now-vanished settlement of Majorville). Quite like a wheel in design, its massive central stone cairn, 10 metres in diameter and nearly two metres high, is connected to an outer rim by 26 or 28 "spokes." Again there are signs of interference: initials formed by rearrangement of some of the surface stones. However, the cairn itself, though known to local ranchers since the turn of the last century, had not been plundered when archaeologist Brian Calder began investigations in 1971, stripping the stones off, layer by layer. Unlike the British Block Cairn, this one had been built gradually over time. Here the ages of the layers could be identified by different kinds of projectile points and by other dating methods, such as obsidian hydration and carbon 14 testing. Nearly 3,000 artifacts were recovered, the oldest ones at the bottom, the youngest at the top, as one might expect.

Analysis showed that the cairn had been started 5,000 years ago (1,000 years before Stonehenge and 500 years before the pyramids at Giza), and had been used and added to by six successive cultures right up to the time of European contact, though there was a clearly defined thousand-year gap in its use, from 2,000 to 3,000 years ago (corresponding to the time of the Altithermal heat wave that forced the buffalo north). Among the findings were 500 projectile points, bones and other artifacts stained with sacred red ochre, and several buffalo stones or iniskim, magical fetishes used to call the buffalo near. Brian Calder believed it to have been a centre for ceremonies to ensure the fertility of the buffalo and for success in the hunt. Was the great perimeter ring there from the first, or added later? No dating tests were done. Were the ring and the spokes somehow related to the rituals? There are always more questions

Categories

Examining the design of all the 46 known medicine wheels in Alberta, John Brumley found that they could be fitted into eight configurations, each one serving a specific purpose. A burial lodge, for example, fits into his Category Number 4. Ian Brace, curator of archaeology at the Royal Saskatchewan Museum, has a different scheme for the medicine wheels of his province. He has divided them into four categories relating to use: burial, surrogate burial, fertility symbol, and medicine hunting. The first two would seem to equate with Brumley's Type 4.

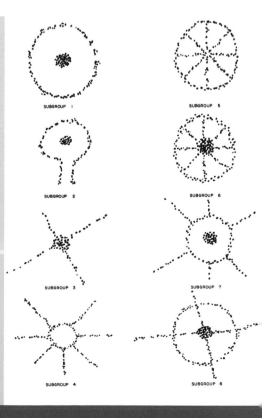

SUBGROUP 1

SUBGROUP 2

SUBGROUP 3

SUBGROUP 4

SUBGROUP 5

SUBGROUP 6

SUBGROUP 7

SUBGROUP 8

Ellis

Another site on the Suffield reserve is more of a starburst than a wheel: Long stone lines radiate from a central tipi-size ring, and there are 13 other tipi rings nearby. The site is on a promontory overlooking the deep valley of the South Saskatchewan River, and to archaeologist John Brumley it seemed most likely to be a burial lodge. Inside the small central ring were found the bones of an old man, along with butchered bison bones, stone tools and points, and the remains of a sharpened oak stake that had been painted blue and driven into the centre. The wood was dated between AD 1200 and 1500. The human bones were as deeply buried as the perimeter stones, and were very well preserved, suggesting they had been placed on the prairie surface at the same time.

If it was indeed a burial lodge, then the bones were probably those of a powerful chief who had been placed inside his tipi after death, a practice reported by plains First Nations people. Then the tipi would have been closed tightly, tied down to the central stake for extra security, and abandoned. Radiating lines of stones were placed around the tipi to denote its purpose and to show respect. A hide tipi, securely fastened to the earth by stones and a stake, would last a long time before wind and weather tore it down and prairie soil sifted over its contents. This would explain why the human bones were so well preserved.

Determining the age of medicine wheels is difficult. Most stand on hilltops, swept by the ceaseless prairie wind and unlikely to be buried very deeply by soil, so that dating by stratigraphy (the depositing of soil in layers) is impossible. Lichen growth is a method that has been tried, but lichens grow infinitessimally slowly, the rate governed by climate and orientation. Lichen growth at the site can be measured (one needs at least 10 years for this) and the rate extrapolated back to give age, assuming the rocks at the site were lichen-free when placed.

Lichens can be used to date a medicine wheel and other stone sites.

Boulder flow dating measures chemical changes in the soil under the stones brought about by rain flowing over them after placement, but this can only be used to measure age relative to another feature on the same site—the rim of the wheel to the spokes, for example. Archaeologists have established a series of dates based on known chronological ages of certain styles of projectile point, and this is still a prime method, but testing of organic materials buried within the wheel, such as the wooden stake at Ellis, gives the surest dates.

Aerial view of the Ellis medicine wheel.
John Brumley photograph.

Precious Stones

Looking at the stones on ancient cairns, each one carried by hand for who knows how many days, one is impressed by their variety. Not ordinary prairie cobbles, they seem to have been chosen for their beauty: bright colours, intricate veining, swirls of sedimentary layering, or crystalline sparkles. Perhaps, in the minds of their carriers, the stones exerted some kind of magic allure and cried out to be taken to a sacred place. Today, the stones are further enhanced by the designs of coloured lichens. Lichen grows very slowly; its presence alone denotes great age.

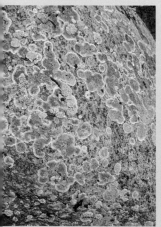

Medicine Wheel Astronomy

Archaeologists sift through the dust of the past to find answers to the medicine wheel mysteries, but scientists of other disciplines have entered the field with theories of their own. One hypothesis is that the constructions were observatories, built specifically to point to the sunrise and sunset of both summer and winter solstices. Some may also have marked the positions on the horizon of the heliacal risings (when they are first seen) of certain bright stars.

Astronomer John Eddy, working at the Bighorn medicine wheel on Medicine Mountain in Wyoming, found that a line drawn from an outlying cairn, to the centre of the central cairn, pointed to within three degrees of the summer solstice sunrise, the day allotted for sun dance ceremonies. Other cairn alignments were found to mark the risings of the bright stars Aldebaran, Sirius, and Rigel. The Bighorn wheel (probably the most like a wheel of any, with 28 radiating spokes and a well-defined rim) is, he pointed out, similar in design to the Cheyenne sun dance lodge, which has a central post and 28 radiating rafters. Others suggest the 28 spokes represent the days in a lunar month or the 28 ribs of a bison.

Sunset at Sundial Hill creates an eerie glow.

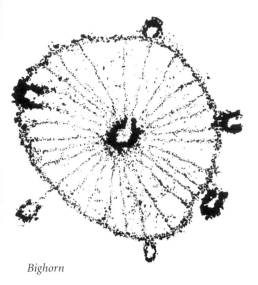

Bighorn

Moose Mountain

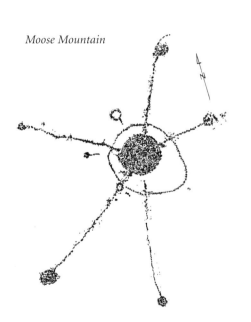

Eddy compared his findings from Bighorn to other medicine wheels in North America (most of them are found in Alberta), examining, in particular, those with lines, or "spokes." Many seemed to be aligned with the summer solstice sunrise and even with some of the same bright stars. When he looked at the Moose Mountain medicine wheel, on the highest point of land in southeastern Saskatchewan, he amazed even himself. Though twice the size of Bighorn and shaped quite differently, the long radiating spokes and associated small cairns were identically aligned to those at Bighorn. "The six cairns on each wheel can be placed into a one-on-one correspondence, almost as if the same building plan had been used for both," he reported.

Could this be true? Could there have been some ancient architect who masterminded the two constructions hundreds of kilometres apart? Michael Wilson of the University of Calgary went to Bighorn to see if archaeological evidence could add anything to the puzzle. He found that since the stones of the wheel's spokes overlapped the deeply buried edges of the cairn, the central cairn was older than the spokes (by several hundred years), and thus it was unlikely that spokes and cairns together had been planned as part of an observatory. In the excavated portion of the cairn, only utilitarian items were found, suggesting something other than ceremonial or astronomical function. In addition, Eddy's measurements had depended on there being a sighting pole in the central cairn, but no sign of this was found.

Astronomer David Rodger of the H.R. MacMillan Planetarium in Vancouver once went to film the sunrise

at the summer solstice at the Moose Mountain medicine wheel for a planetarium show. When he stood on the sighting cairn he found his view of the sunrise blocked by the central cairn. The sun rose 25 minutes late and six degrees south of the solstice line! What had seemed likely from a flat drawing was impossible, given the topography. The cairn is on the apex of the hill; the spokes slope downwards.

Astronomical studies have also been conducted at the 5,000-year-old Majorville medicine wheel, which sits on the top of one of three hills above the Bow River. There are many cairns and rings within three kilometres of the site, and several of the cairn alignments accurately mark the cardinal directions. After more than 20 years of study, University of Alberta professors Gordon and Phyllis Freeman have reached the conclusion that the Majorville medicine wheel is a rayed centrepiece of a huge temple to the sun, moon, and morning star (Venus) and that various stone sighting lines, ranging in lengths from 50 metres to 4,000 metres, mark the positions of sunrise and sunset of the solstices and equinoxes. The accuracy of the solstice lines is better than 0.2 degrees. The temple, they contend, extends about 100 square kilometres. They also note that the area is rich in other First Nations sites: There are three tipi ring villages, buffalo wallows and traps, and at least one buffalo jump in the vicinity.

Exploring the Medicine Wheels

Because medicine wheels are still considered sacred to the native peoples and the simple stones of their construction are easy to pilfer and to rearrange, the sites are, for the most part, so well protected that they remain secret. Most are on private land and not easily reached—except by long dirt tracks and with the owner's permission. There are, however, some that can be visited.

Sundial Hill

This was the very first wheel that I encountered, and coincidentally it was the subject of the first published account of a medicine wheel in Canada. Surveyor George Dawson in his 1855 *Geological and Natural History of Canada* reported: "A point of interest to the Indians in this region (southern Alberta) is that called Sun-dial Hill ... There is here a cairn with concentric circles of stones and radiating lines ... It is ... regarded with much reverence."

The Sundial Hill medicine wheel east of Carmangay, Alberta, is one of the few that the public are allowed to visit on their own. Fenced from marauding cattle, it has an interpretive board that explains its age and possible use. But there are no highway signs, and to drive near, one needs a sturdy vehicle. Like most medicine wheels, it tops a hill with commanding views in all directions, overlooking the incised coulee of the Little Bow River and the adjacent reservoir. Smaller hills lie to the north and west, several topped by small rock clusters, and there are many tipi rings in the area. Sundial's central cairn has been plundered (early settlers believed the cairns to have been burial mounds and hoped to find valuable artifacts), but the rocks have been more or less returned to their original position, leaving a depression in the centre where a tough gooseberry bush has taken hold. In this

The sound of the meadowlark, one of the joys of summer, at a medicine wheel.

Travel Info

To get to Sundial Hill, drive Secondary Highway 522 east from the town of Carmangay for about 27 kilometres, over the swelling hump of Blackspring Ridge, until you can see the blue dimple of Little Bow reservoir ahead. Turn south (a small white arrow points the way) following a fence along a road marked "Robin Compressor" for about a kilometre. The road swings left at a cattle-guard and the medicine wheel track lies directly ahead. If you look carefully, one of the hills has a small hump on it. Follow the rough track for about 1.5 kilometres to the medicine wheel fence (You might choose to walk from the cattle-guard). This is grazing land, so don't spook the cattle. An excellent sign at the medicine wheel fence gives information. Treat the site with reverence and don't disturb any of the stones. Enjoy the view, and the flowers. Try to feel something of the power of the place.

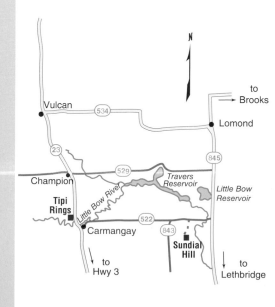

At Sundial Hill, sky and stones seem to swirl together.

Purple fleabane.

bush, one can sometimes find prayer flags or a bunch of sage, denoting a native visit. Around the cairn are two concentric circles of rocks broken at the south to form an entrance corridor.

It's a beautiful spot, particularly in June when the grass is thick and spangled with wildflowers. When I was there, spiky cactuses showed off their deep magenta blooms and meadowlarks called. Small clouds galloped across the sky, their shadows dappling the grass so that the landscape itself seemed on the move. I stayed until sunset, a bewitching time anywhere, and had planned to stay the night. But the wind made strange noises, and in the silence between gusts, the sound of my heart was suddenly loud. My skin prickled. This was indeed a place of power. I left before dark, unwilling to relinquish the world I knew.

Moose Mountain

This is probably the largest and certainly the most famous of the medicine wheels in Saskatchewan, mostly because of its connection with astronomical theories. It is also on one of the most beautiful sites. Moose Mountain Provincial Park protects a special area, a large upland of wooded serenity and many lakes, popular for summer recreation. West of the park, on the Pheasant Rump Reserve of the Nakota First Nations, the highest point of the uplands was chosen by the ancients for the sprawling medicine wheel that has given rise to so much academic speculation. First recorded in 1896 in a book called *Canadian Savage Folk,* the site was commented on by author J. Maclean: "The Indians know nothing of the origin of these lines and cairns but they state that they were made by the spirit of the winds."

Some of the long spokes of Moose Mountain medicine wheel end in small cairns, believed to signal sighting lines to the solstice.

There are five long spokes radiating from a huge hub of stones that sits off-centre in its oval "rim," rather like the yolk in an egg when it is hard-boiled and cut in half. The shape is difficult to see from the ground because of the topography and the long grass.

Armand McArthur, a Nakota tribal elder, lives just down the hill from the wheel, and he and his dog walk up there often, usually just to "sit and think." He drove me up to the wheel on a shadowless morning in June with clouds covering the usually blue canvas of sky and "the spirit of the winds" cold and fierce. He walked a distance away by himself, faced west, muttering quietly, then threw a pinch of something onto the cairn. Tobacco, he said, an offering. We walked around the cairn, examining the closely set double stones of the circle and the long, widely spread arms of the spokes that end in cairns, one in a definite horseshoe shape. Among the pile of stones in the cairn are straggly bushes of wild gooseberry and raspberry, the seeds brought up perhaps by birds.

Travel Info

If you want to visit, phone the Pheasant Rump Nakota Nation Office (306-462-2002) north of the little town of Kisby on Saskatchewan Highway 13.

The central cairn of the Moose Mountain medicine wheel is huge and colourful. The outer ring is easier to see in spring and fall when the grass is short.

He told me the colours of the medicine wheel, how north was white, east red, south yellow for the sun, and west black for the thunderbird. Everyone is born with a special colour, he said, and to know what this is, one simply imagines one's favourite. Mine happens to be blue, which doesn't fit into the medicine wheel spectrum. We talked about this and other subjects bordering on the supernatural, and Armand pointed across the coulee to where there were many tipi rings. It was too cold and windy to stay long but I asked to come back again, this time with some tobacco of my own.

A month later, when I returned, Armand suggested that I go up to the site by myself. A typical Saskatchewan summer's day, the sky was blue, the sun hot, but still the wind blew, though this time it was warm. The central cairn was wreathed in the brilliant yellow of mustard flowers, and a strident eastern kingbird nested in the bushes. Alone, it was a high and heady experience, listening to whispers and watching the shadows of small clouds move across the juicy greens of the summer landscape. The land seemed to ripple with life. I wondered what architect had designed this place and how many people had carried stones, from who knows how far away, up to the cairn. I stayed for an hour or so, then self-consciously sprinkled some tobacco on the cairn, as I had seen Armand do, and then I left, feeling somehow ennobled.

Majorville

The Majorville medicine wheel does not reveal itself easily to the visitor: At first glance it is simply a heap of stones, but an aerial view or a plan will show the full intricacies of its design with a cairn, an outer ring, 26 or 28 spokes, and several disturbed effigies. The stones of the cairn seem particularly colourful and I noticed a small thunder-egg, or geode, filled with crystals. Had this been placed by the ancient builders, or brought recently, as an offering? There are several small outlying clusters of stones, their colours made even more flamboyant by brilliant lichens. One of these, quite far down on the north side of the hill, seems to be the focus of present-day attention: When I was there, a cruciform figure made from sagebrush wrapped in red fabric had been propped between the red and green boulders. It looked to me a bit like a primitive scarecrow. The place is superb, with a great sweeping view down to the curvaceous Bow River, a blue snake far below. One can well believe that it is the focus of a grand sun temple.

It seems fitting that a visit to such a powerful place requires a fairly complicated drive and the use of a four-wheel-drive vehicle, or at least the high clearance of a pickup truck. I was first taken there by Siksika elder

The Majorville Cairn sits high and lonely above the Bow River.

Clifford Many Guns via a complicated series of oil exploration tracks from the non-existent settlement of Majorville (it's still marked on the map). He knew the area from past hunting trips and was surprised to see the cairn now protected by a fence. We climbed to the top of the hill, and, facing the cairn, he muttered prayers to the spirits there. Some of the prayers were for me, he said, to guard me in my travels.

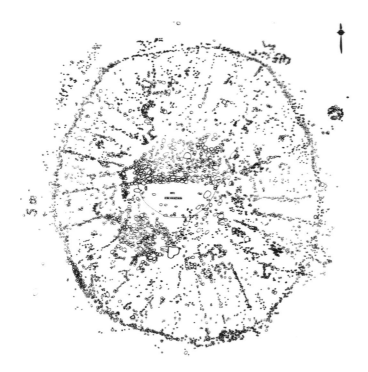

The intricate structure of the Majorville Cairn, with its 28 spokes, emerges from the detailed plan. Some believe it is a sun temple.
Courtesy of John Brumley.

Travel Info

Later that summer, I was told of an easier route that starts from Highway 539, 17 km west of Bow City (which is southwest of Brooks). Take rural road 185 (beside the Armada Gas Plant) north for 10 km, then turn right at a corral (a road does go straight here) and follow a fence line along Township Road 182. At 13.3 km where the road almost ends, turn left (north) across a cattle-guard (road 183). Continue under a power line, across a second cattle-guard, and beside a sign marking the site of the former Amethyst School. Just beyond the school site, look left for a prominent buffalo-rubbing stone, shiny with centuries of use. Continue along the track, past a sign for the Lomond Grazing Association and up an alarmingly steep incline. At the top, keep a lookout for a small hill to the east (right) that has a small cairn on top—more like a little nest of colourful rocks—and a beautiful view of the Bow River; it's well worth the short hike to the top. Back on the track, in less than a kilometre you will come to the fence that protects the medicine wheel. Again, there's an excellent interpretive sign. (Total: 22.5 km from the highway.)

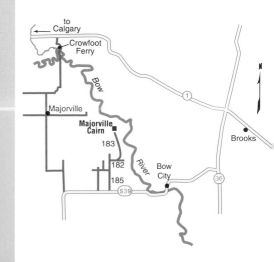

Roy Rivers

Another medicine wheel with a stupendous view sits almost astride the Saskatchewan-Alberta border east of the town of Empress. On the highest point of the ridge overlooking the confluence of the Red Deer and South Saskatchewan rivers, this wheel has a central stone cairn

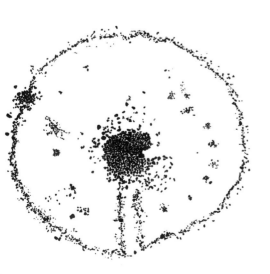

surrounded by a single ring with an entrance "corridor." There is one small cairn on the circumference and several clusters, one perhaps a disturbed effigy, inside the circle. The stones of the construction are particularly beautiful, multi-coloured and patterned with lichens. Along the ridge, an elongated nest of stones suggests a vision quest site, and on a slightly lower bench sit two tipi rings. Hundreds of other rings can still be found on the prairie below: The river valley was a favourite wintering spot of the Blackfoot, the earliest known inhabitants of the area.

Roy Rivers was the first to homestead on this property in 1916, and I was guided to the site by his granddaughter, Velma Booker, who speaks fondly of running up to the medicine wheel on her way home from school. It's a fairly steep walk from the grain fields below, but once there, it is hard to pull yourself away from the view, and Velma obviously delights in pointing out the landmarks and recounting the history. Somewhere near the river forks below lies the site, described in historical records but still undiscovered, of the Hudson's Bay Company's Chesterfield House trading post, established by Peter Fidler in 1800.

Aerial view.
Photograph by George Tosh.

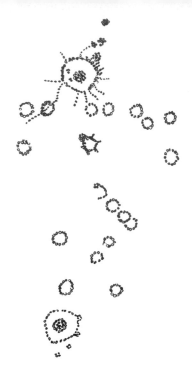

Miner's (Bar Diamond)

On the high valley rim of the Red Deer River near Bindloss, a short drive northwest of Empress, two medicine wheels sit amid a constellation of 38 tipi rings, several cairns, and the possible representations of a turtle and a snake. There are rings, clusters of stones, and small cairns just about everywhere on this stretch of unbroken prairie, and it is difficult to distinguish the different configurations, particularly if the grass is long. The two medicine wheels are very different. One cairn is surrounded by a single, closed ring with square appendages like ears on the northwest rim. The other is a strange arrangement: a central cairn surrounded by a stone ring with an east-facing entrance funnel and several attached, wavering spokes of different lengths. The longest spoke bisects a double-walled stone circle. Inside the main ring are two other small cairns, and just outside its western edge lie two larger ones. The small snake effigy, its head a

small rock cluster, lies about midway between the two wheels, with the "turtle" about 25 metres away.

The two wheels are about 120 metres apart, and as I walked between them, carefully avoiding thick mats of blooming cactus, I wondered whether both had served the same purpose, and if so, were they both used at the same time? I also noticed that many of the tipi rings seemed to be double-walled, as if this had been a winter camp.

The heart of a cactus replicates the sacred circle of the medicine wheel.

Travel Info

This astonishing site, set in a scenic position of high command above the river, lies on land belonging to the Bar Diamond Ranch, which runs 650 head of cattle on its 14,000 hectares. Owners Bob Lyon, Jim Horn, and Carol Hern have turned the isolated log ranch house, built in 1902, into a comfortable riverside guest lodge, a base for summer jet-boat trips on the South Saskatchewan River and for fall upland bird hunting. The lodge is also available for "secret hideouts" for wildlife viewing (pronghorn, elk, and eagles) as well as tours to the medicine wheel site, an opportunity not to be missed. Their Web site: www.albertawesternuplands.com or phone: 1-800-375-7286.

Rumsey

Less than 10 kilometres southwest of the village of Rumsey, what is known locally as Stonepile Hill dominates the horizon. The furthest north of all known Alberta medicine wheels, it consists of a stone cairn surrounded by two concentric circles and the disturbed effigies of what were once recorded as a man, a dog, and a horse. Today the Rumsey site is an example of a site almost destroyed by human thoughtlessness. The cairn, which was at one time some 3 metres high, was torn apart in the 1930s, probably by artifact hunters, and the effigies have been rearranged. Early settlers reported that at one time a dead spruce tree had been propped up in the cairn centre for a local landmark.

Wild geranium.

Despite the vandalism, the site was professionally examined in 1961 by an archaeological crew from the Glenbow Museum, which excavated half of the cairn. They found quantities of stone arrowheads, potsherds, glass beads, and fragments of a stone pipe. The base of the cairn had been lined with red ochre. The crew rebuilt the

*Is there a stone man
hidden in the sagebrush?*

plundered cairn as best they could. The site is still very
beautiful and quite easy to find. I went there with Kevin
Hronek, curator of the Trochu and District Museum,
who had phoned around for directions. We were both
amazed by the fine view, the huge cairn, and the numbers
of disturbed stone arrangements. We failed to find the
stone man, though we could very well have been looking
at it among the scatter of stones. Cattle range the land and
cow pats litter the ground, adding to the confusion.

Travel Info

To reach Rumsey Cairn, take Highway 585 east
from Trochu and cross the Tolman Bridge over the
Red Deer River. Turn right on Rural Road 213 for
6.5 km; then turn left on Township Road 330
and head up the hill towards a communications
tower. Park beside a commemorative sign for the
pioneer school Two Valley Hills. There's a gate
nearby and a rough track across the field. Head
for the high point, being careful not to scare the
cattle. The grass is long around the cairn, and
the circles and the disturbed effigies are hard to
see. Try to arrive for the sunset. The view is
superb and the atmosphere electric.

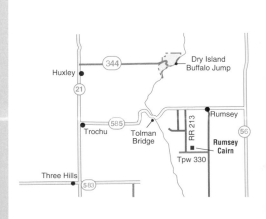

Circles of Ceremony

Some stone circles found on the prairie are large, far too large for a tipi ring, but they fit none of the classifications for a medicine wheel. Archaeologists have dubbed them "ceremonial circles" and suggest a purpose similar to those at a medicine wheel. Some of these large rings have lines of rocks running through their centres like dividers, sometimes following the cardinal directions, either north-south or east-west. In Saskatchewan, one large stone circle (diameter 8 metres) sits on a hilltop surrounded by a cluster of other rings varying in size from 2.5 to 6.9 metres. This large ring is sliced roughly into two by an inner dividing line. Another stone configuration (it is more kidney-shaped than circular) is huge—27 metres by 20 metres—far larger than the surrounding tipi rings, and has a line of stones dividing the inner space into two, uneven-sized portions, 1/3 and 2/3. Each of the two "rooms" has a doorway. In Alberta, it seems that most

Huge "ceremonial circle" near Big Muddy.
Courtesy of the Royal Saskatchewan Museum.

bisected stone circles are of tipi size; four of the stone rings around the Majorville Cairn, for example, are divided, as are those at other sites.

While no one can explain the purpose of these divided rings, it has been suggested that they could be indicators of shamans' tents used for the widespread and well-documented "shaking tent" ceremony. This involved the ritual invocation of spirits summoned for help or advice or to predict the future, a bit like the oracles of the Old World. The inner lines of stones would have helped support a wall of hides or blankets, behind which the "oracle" was hidden. From one Piikani account: "During the rite, people are all around in the tipi. A curtain is put over a part of the interior … and the medium sits behind the curtain. During the performance noises are heard 'inside' and everything moves, including the tent itself." There is no documented evidence for partitioning the tipi for any other reason.

There are also stone alignments on open ground, not associated with buffalo jumps or animal impoundments, that seem to have been made simply to partition areas, perhaps the sacred from the mundane. At one such site, a single large cairn on a promontory overlooking the Red Deer River is backed by a line of four smaller cairns and, 30 metres away, two curving lines of rock that overlap in the centre to permit a narrow entrance. Not generally considered a medicine wheel, the site nevertheless does have a ceremonial feel to it. And a medicine wheel on an isolated spur of land above the South Saskatchewan River is protected along the neck of the spur by 57 boulders, a line perhaps built to stop bison from running into the area, or to distinguish a sacred area from the rest of the prairie.

Near Pakowki Lake in southern Alberta, one mystifying cluster of stone circles, none of which has the typical tipi doorway, includes a large ring of roughly 11 metres in diameter inset with a smaller five-metre circle. Is this also a ceremonial site?

"Weeping eye" glyphstone. Glenbow C261-1

Stone Effigies

Possible turtle effigy at Herschel.

Opposite: Cabri Lake effigy.
George Tosh photograph.

Dorothy effigy.
Courtesy of the Heritage Resource Management Branch, Alberta.

Perhaps even more mysterious than medicine wheels are the outlines in stone of men or animals that lie on grassy highlands throughout Alberta and Saskatchewan. While again difficult to date, they are generally ascribed to people of the same era as those who created the medicine wheels. The formations most likely had some ceremonial or spiritual significance in the past, and they are considered sacred sites by native people today. Offerings of tobacco, sage, and coloured cloths can often be found nearby.

Made of small glacial boulders, the effigies that still exist are mostly of men, but there are several turtles, snakes, a badger, a salamander, and one, only one, buffalo. The shapes are difficult to see from the ground, and one is tempted to speculate whether they were made only for higher beings to observe. The stones that delineate them are easy to pry up and move about, and several effigies have been disturbed. Like medicine wheels, they should be treated with respect.

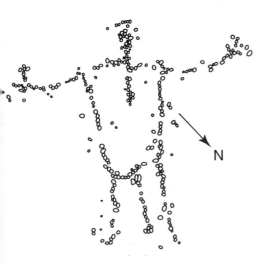

Napi Figures

Fifteen stone effigies of men have been found in the grasslands of Alberta and Saskatchewan. Eleven of these are very similar in design, with rectangular box bodies, upraised arms with fingers, sturdy legs, feet turned sideways, heart-lines, and prominent sex organs. Six of them are aligned with their heads to the west. In this position, if they could sit

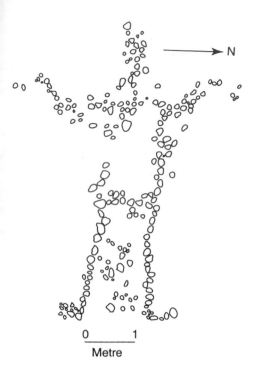

up they would face east, just as a man lying in a tipi would have faced the rising sun through the doorway. In Blackfoot history, these recumbent male figures are said to represent the resting places of Old Man or Napi, who formed the world and everything on it. In *Blackfoot Lodge Tales,* published in 1907, George Grinnell told of the Old Man "travelling about, south of here, making the people. He came from the south, travelling north, making animals and birds as he passed along … Being tired, he went up on a little hill and lay down to rest. As he lay on his back, stretched out on the ground, with arms extended, he marked himself out with stones—the shape of his body, head, legs, arms, and everything. There you can see the rock today." The Napi figures are regarded as sacred sites by today's Blackfoot (the Siksika, Piikani, and Kainai people).

Above: Napi figure at British Block Cairn. Bottom left: in Dinosaur Provincial Park. Right: Ross effigy. (Is the cairn his head?) All courtesy of the Heritage Resource Management Branch, Alberta.

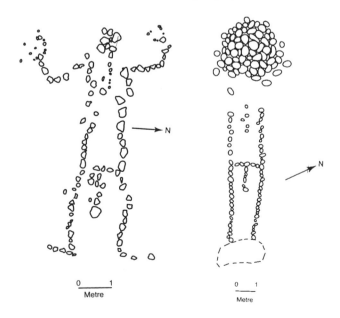

Wild Man Butte

The figure on Wild Man Butte, a high ridge south of the Coteau Lakes in southeastern Saskatchewan, is a good example of vandalism. Today, the man has a face like a grinning Halloween pumpkin, a tail, and a huge penis. When the land was first leased in 1914 he was already in place, the stones of his outline apparently deeply embedded. He remained apparently untouched until examined and

Wild Man on the butte overlooking the Coteau Lakes is hard to distinguish in the spring grass, and with a storm brewing.

Aerial view of floured figure.
· George Tosh photograph.

The Wild Man lies on a shoulder of the butte seen on the horizon above fields of canola.

mapped by archaeologists in 1961. Then came historical evidence of tampering. A miner called William Clandening passed this way from Ontario en route to the Montana goldmines, and in 1863 he penned a report on the hilltop effigy. The man he saw then had no face or tail and was carrying a bow-and-arrow in his right hand. Obviously, the effigy had undergone a transformation.

It was late in the day when I toiled up the grassy hillside to the Wild Man site, and a black summer storm was threatening. The Coteau Lakes were filled with waterfowl and a flock of pelicans stayed just too far away to photograph. Around the lakes, fields were brilliant with flowering canola (or was it mustard?), and as I climbed I had to step carefully around huge mats of cactus. On a flat part of the ridge, just below the highest point, the Wild Man was stretched comfortably, head to the west, just as if he were lying in his tipi. With the summer grass so long, it was hard to see him except bit by bit. But I knew what he looked like. I stared into his eyes. He may have been tampered with, but he was still magnificent.

I stayed with the man—was he Napi?—keeping him company as the storm rumbled close and lightning flashed and scribbled on the blackboard sky. The first huge raindrops were reason enough for me to run down the hill to the shelter of my car. When the storm blew away and the sun came out, there was a magnificent rainbow. It is always worth seeking out these sacred sites, if only for the great landscapes and for the possibility of wonderful weather effects.

Travel Info
If they are assured of your serious intent and respect for native places, the village office at Minton, Saskatchewan, might provide directions to this powerful and intensely beautiful place, which lies east of Highway 6 near the Montana border.

Cabri Lake Man

While some of the stone effigies have been rearranged since the first settlers found them, there is one case of wholesale disappearance or kidnap, followed by clever sleuthing, discovery, and eventual replacement. The Napi effigy at Cabri Lake lies on high ground near land that is farmed by Ted Douglas of Eatonia. An amateur archaeologist, Ted keeps good watch over the figure (at one time from his small plane), and he likes to take visitors to see it. One day, the man was gone; only bare spots in the grass marked where he had lain. It was as if the man had simply walked away. Telephone detective work revealed what had happened. The figure had been scientifically removed for safekeeping by the Saskatchewan Museum of Natural History (now the Royal Saskatchewan Museum), which had marked each stone and planned to resurrect him on museum grounds. Douglas and other members of the Saskatchewan Archaeological Society protested,

Richardson's ground squirrels.
George Tosh photograph.

and eventually the man was brought back and replaced, stone by stone, exactly where he had lain for, probably, thousands of years.

I met Douglas some years back and he took me to the site, first in his plane—aerial views (see page 113) are definitely the best way to appreciate these effigies—then in his pickup. The stone man looked none the worse for his moving experience. Unlike other Napi figures, this one faces west. Whoever made him took extra pains to

make him realistic. His thighs are solid, big ,and beefy. He has a heart-shaped stone for a heart and two fat kidneys, and genitals that are all there. He wears a feather on his head and he seems to be dancing, one leg bent, arms in the air. One of his feet looks like a claw—perhaps he was a kind of eagle-man. I can well understand why Ted has taken this dancing man under his wing. He has personality.

Cabri Lake was named after the French word for "antelope."

The man effigy may be the most impressive of the sites that Ted looks after at Cabri Lake but there are many others, including hundreds of tipi rings, possible eagle-trapping or vision quest sites, long enigmatic lines of stones that seemingly lead nowhere, a beautiful buffalo rubbing stone, and even a pictograph rock. He has a theory that some of the constructions, built like shallow wells, were fire pits used to signal band members in the area, perhaps to let them know when game or enemies were approaching, or perhaps to summon them to the Napi ceremonies. Douglas discovered many of the sites while flying over the land in the early morning after a light snowfall. The first sun melted the snow on the stones, providing clear negative images, black on white. (When archaeologists photograph sites from the air, they first have the stones dusted with flour, a white-on-black view.)

Winter aerial at Cabri Lake.
George Tosh photograph.

Travel Info

The area west of Cabri Lake, mostly still unbroken, is being considered for special status as an archaeological preserve to protect further encroachment from oil wells or farms. All the sites that Ted Douglas has found and guarded so well are being carefully mapped and recorded with the Global Positioning System by Saskatchewan Heritage Resources.

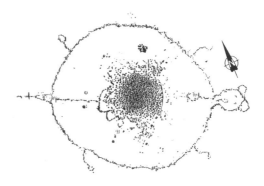

Plan of the Minton Turtle. You can't see much except the central bushy cairn. Does it even look like a turtle at all?

Turtles

This turtle effigy near Minton, Saskatchewan, can't seem to make up its mind whether it is a medicine wheel or a turtle. It has a huge, bushy cairn surrounded by a symmetrical circle of stones almost 30 metres in diameter, just like a wheel. However, there are four legs, a tail, some suggestion of carapace marking, and a very questionable turtle head, with two Mickey Mouse ears, two eyes, and a snout. (One archaeologist thinks it represents a badger.) An outlying cairn and a line with a small sunburst at one end appear to mark the summer solstice sunrise. The central cairn itself was looted a long time ago, but the site is still considered sacred. When I visited it last in blazing July, the grass was long, obscuring most of the stones, and in the bushes of the cairn hung coloured prayer flags that denoted a native visit, perhaps for a vision quest. The figure's head faces southeast, towards Napi sleeping on Wild Man Butte.

Plan of Turtle Number Two—much more like a turtle.

Turtle #2

This Saskatchewan turtle is smaller (10 metres by 7 metres) and neater than the first, the grass around it less shaggy. It faces south over a lovely landscape of rolling coulees and today lies behind a closed wire fence; a set of viewing bleachers gives a better photographic angle. (Most of these effigies can be seen properly only from above.) But the fence, while protecting the figure from vandalism, also detracts from the atmosphere of the place. It puts the turtle into a zoo enclosure, for people to gawk at. One can only regret that such protection is considered necessary.

Photograph before the little turtle was enclosed behind a fence.
Courtesy of the Royal Saskatchewan Museum.

Turtles (the Western painted variety) are found on the prairies only in waters that drain to the Mississippi. In native lore they are symbols of fertility and longevity. Blackfoot girls were urged to "be industrious like the spider, wise like the turtle, and cheerful like the lark."

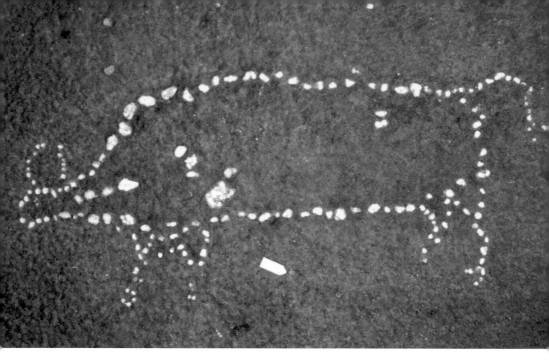

Bison Effigy

Close to the Montana border near Big Beaver,
Saskatchewan, the finely wrought figure of a stone buffalo
browses on the prairie grass. This is the only known effigy
of a buffalo on the North American grasslands, which is
strange given the importance of this animal to the lives and
sustenance of the first inhabitants. Seen from above, its
stones covered with flour for definition, the buffalo effigy is
an immaculate, carefully crafted facsimile. It has a hump, a
curving tail, horns, a heartline, and several big stones
suggesting internal organs. From ground level, the figure is
so long (more than 11 metres) that one needs a fisheye lens
to photograph it. It is hard to see the entire effigy.

*The same figure from
ground level.*

Remains of an active sweat lodge below the hill.

The small cairn at the buffalo's feet provides support for a tall wood pole, and when I visited in July, this was adorned with tiny bags of sage and other herbs while several pieces of coloured cloth flapped in the breeze like Tibetan prayer flags. The site is sacred to today's native people, many of whom cross the nearby border to attend the site. Below the buffalo hill are well-used sweat lodges, and there are several clear tipi rings nearby.

Symbols of native reverence, prayer flags, fly at the bison effigy site.

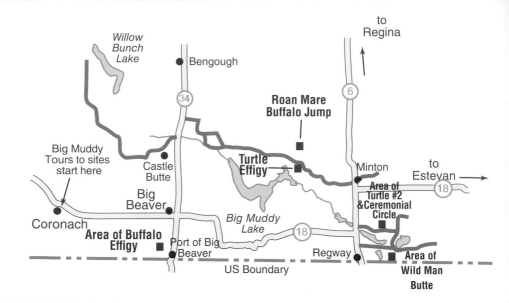

Where to See the Effigies

The Minton turtle is easy to find, lying on a road allowance very near to the turning for the Roan Mare Buffalo Jump. From Highway 6, take the grid road leading west from Minton and follow its zigzag course for about 6 or 7 km. By an oil well depot, a small, handmade sign points southwest to a short trail (the first part is often wet and thick with mosquitoes) that leads to the top of a knoll overlooking Big Muddy Valley. The bushes of the central cairn are prominent on the skyline.

Turtle Effigy #2, now inside a fence.

Both the small turtle (#2) and the bison effigy can be visited with a guide from the nearby town of Coronach, Saskatchewan.

The road through the Big Muddy badlands.

Castle Butte.

Big Muddy

Big Muddy Tours runs from the Coronach town office, and takes visitors into the badlands to see the effigies and other native sites, including a huge ceremonial circle and sweat lodges. Also on the tour are outlaw caves, a historic school-house, semi-ghost towns, and natural scenic spots. Transportation is by minibus; the guides are well versed, the cost minimal. The four-hour tours usually run twice a day from May through September, or by request. Check the website: www.coronach.ca; or e-mail: townoffice@coronach.ca.

Rock Art

a

Opposite page and below: ancient art from Writing-on-Stone.

Early mankind everywhere in the world has used rock for artistic and spiritual expression—in caves, on cliffs, and on single stones. Because stone endures, rock art sites provide vivid links to past ways of life: the practical and the arcane. In them we catch faint glimpses of the first people's very different views of the cosmos, their rituals and their beliefs, their fears and their dreams. And we inch a little closer to understanding them.

Throughout the Canadian short-grass plains, there are scores of rock sites encrypted with ancient pictures and designs, some of them inscribed (petroglyphs), some of them painted (pictographs). While the buffalo hunters had no formal writing, these "pictures" can be construed as messages on stone passing on information that archaeologists are only now beginning to decipher. Some of this iconography is ancient, dating from around 3,000 years ago. Some was executed within historic time. A few panels are thought to represent real events—a sort of newspaper report—while other motifs picture the supernatural, attempting to make solid the ephemeral nature of the dream experience, symbolic records of vision quests. The subject is a fascinating one—whole volumes and many learned texts are devoted to its study.

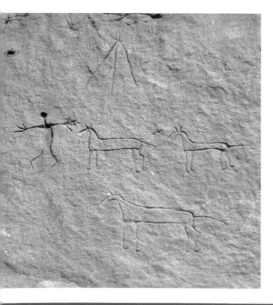

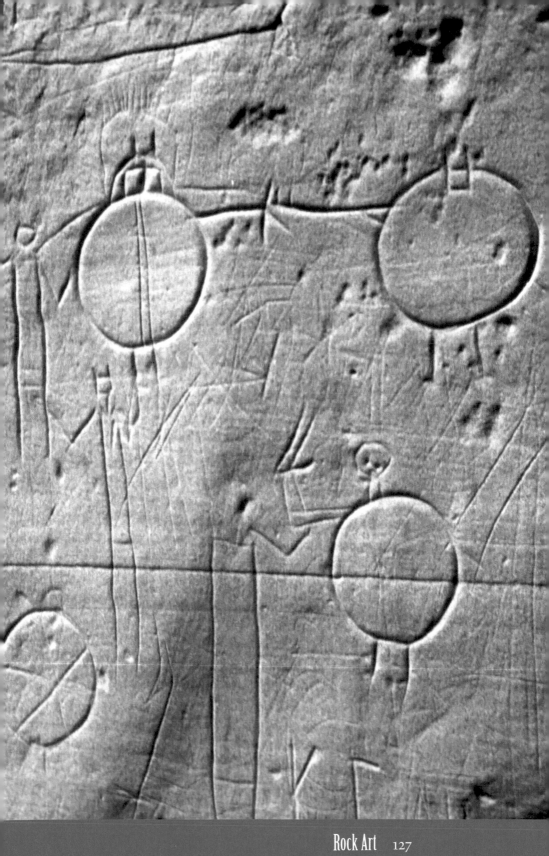

Sunset at Writing-on-Stone, a very special time. The rocks turn to gold, the river to dark blue silk.

Writing-on-Stone

Alberta houses the single most prolific "library" of ancient messages in all of Canada—more than 280 separate pages (panels) in 93 books (sites). On sandstone cliffs above the Milk River, hundreds of ancient carvings portray people and animals, sometimes alone but more often arranged into detailed tableaux, some of which describe historic events. The Writing-on-Stone area is the closest one can come to a "history book" of the first Plains inhabitants. On these rock pages are recorded the changing times of the people who came here, year after year, for centuries. One can well understand why they chose this place: It is hard to imagine a more mystically beautiful landscape, where the sandstone cliffs were easy to carve.

The Milk River is what geologists call an "underfit stream," now too small for the valley it inhabits, a great gorge torn out by torrents of glacial meltwater at the end of the last Ice Age. At the sides of the gorge, pale sandstone has been sculpted by thousands of years of wind

and water to form a spectacularly eerie world of pinnacles, caves, arches, hoodoos, and other formations fantastical, all executed in rock the colour of creamed honey. In summer the river runs clear, with the sparkle of sapphire, and behind it all, the three misty blue humps of the Sweetgrass Hills draw the eye ever upwards.

One can well see how early people, oblivious to the valley's geological history, believed the place to be magical, home to spirits both evil and benign. To the Blackfoot, Writing-on-Stone is known as *Aisinai'pi*, or "It has been written," and their oral tradition asserts that the images were messages scribed on the rocks by spirits and that tribal elders went there to "read" the omens—and to record others of their own. The sacredness of the whole intriguing landscape has always been recognized by native people. Archaeologists believe it was a place for vision quests and that many of the drawings on the cliffs are of a spiritual nature, some going back at least 1,000 years.

Studies of the Milk River art—and there are several—categorize two distinct art forms: iconic and narrative. The iconic, which mostly depicts static figures standing behind huge, circular "power" shields, early forms of weaponry, and boat-shaped animals, was once believed to be earlier than

the narrative form, which portrays active scenes and events that reflect real life. But apparently both forms ran together through the ages, the "power shield" motif appearing alongside horses, for example. Firm dates for these glyphs are hard to establish. Only a rough timeline can be inferred, based on the known introduction of certain items or people to the plains: the bow-and-arrow (by AD 200); the gun (around 1715); the horse (1750); and Europeans (around 1800). Some scientifically reliable dates have emerged from the testing of natural ochre or charcoal paints used in the pictographs. Interestingly, many of the glyphs (the shield-bearing warriors, the V-necked men, and the boat-shaped animals) are

A blood-red sunset and moonrise over the river cliffs.

virtually identical to rock art motifs found in Wyoming, some 750 kilometres to the south.

For the layman, the glyphs themselves are what matters. At Writing-on-Stone, among many strange and unidentifiable figures, can be found a fairly complete bestiary of plains animals: deer, bear, sheep, antelope, snake, fish, bird, turtle, bison (very few considering its importance), and, of course, the horse. There are many horses on the rocks, a sign of the respect and even reverence which the artists had for them. There are single horses protected with archaic armour, displaying brands and metal shoes, and there are whole herds, sometimes drawn with a swift

artistry almost in a kind of shorthand. There are horses with riders, and horses pierced with arrows, and horses hauling travois. Even scenes that have been interpreted as horse-stealing events.

There are also many different portrayals of men: magic men hiding behind their decorated shields (men *with* shields or men *as* shields?), wearing strange headgear and wielding monstrous weapons; men with X-shaped bodies, and rectangular bodies; men engaged in hand-to-hand combat, or sitting astride their new magic weapon, the horse. Here are guns, complete with bullets and trajectories, tipis and huge battle scenes, white men wearing hats, a fort, a gallows, a wagon—the ancient world of the plains in times of transition, seen through ancient eyes.

Protected under a plastic shield beside the Hoodoo Trail at Writing-on-Stone Provincial Park is an enormous battle scene, scratched very delicately on a panel of dark reddish stone. This is said to record the "Retreats up the Hill" battle fought nearby in 1866 between the Piikani and a combined force of Gros Ventres, Cree, and Crow raiders. The Piikani were victorious in this bloody battle, but more than 300 were killed. Of interest is the assertion by storyteller Bird Rattle (who as a boy lived nearby) that the Piikani were given advance notice of this raid because certain of the petroglyphs on this rock appeared overnight as warning and guidance from the spirits.

This painted thunderbird is one of the most aesthetically pleasing—and most sacred—of all the Writing-on-Stone glyphs.
Michael Klassen photograph.

Great horned owls nest in the cliffs.

The battle scene is fading
from the rocks, but
luckily there are detailed
drawings.

The petroglyphs of this ancient battle are hard to see today but a drawing on the nearby explanatory panel shows them well. On one side there is a tipi camp with manned interior fortifications. People are shown inside a central tipi and the village is protected by a line of gunmen, represented by guns spewing bullets. On the other side there are men, guns, a few tipis, and horses pulling travois. And in the centre, a man with a gun confronts another figure wielding a hatchet. The hatchet carrier, said Bird Rattle, was the woman Lone Coup, wife of the Piikani chief Many Horses, attacking the leader of the Gros Ventres, a brave but futile effort: Both she and Many Horses were killed in the battle.

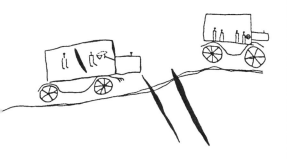

Another fascinating scene shows two early automobiles, apparently travelling in convoy along a road. These were originally thought to be either renderings of early settlers' wagons, or graffiti done at a later time. A recent discovery brought out the truth. In a photograph taken in 1924, the same Piikani elder Bird Rattle (who by then had moved to Browning, Montana, just south of the border), can be seen actually carving the automobile petroglyphs on the rock. He had been driven to Writing-on-Stone by an amateur ethnographer who took photos and left an account of the trip. There were two cars, four people in one, two people in the other—just as the petroglyphs show. Obviously, this tourist trip to Writing-on-Stone was a big event in Bird Rattle's life.

Travel Info

Writing-on-Stone Provincial Park, with its mystical landscape and popular campsite in the willows beside the Milk River, is one of Alberta's very special places. The ever-present threat of vandalism has meant that most of the rock art is now in a protected area, accessible only during guided tours. However, there are several glyphs, including the battle scene, that can be seen from the Hoodoo Trail, which leads visitors through the rock formations and up to the cliff top for a stunning view of the Milk River and the Sweetgrass Hills, a splendid place for sunrises and sunsets when the full magic of the place can be appreciated.

A new Parks Interpretive Centre (opening in the summer of 2005) is built in the round like a ceremonial circle, and looks south and west over the river valley towards the magical Sweetgrass Hills. Like a tipi, its entrance is on the east. The campsite in the willows below is a popular one, and swimming in the river is a summer delight. Tours into the protected areas of the park to see the pictographs take place several times a day during summer.

Also in the park, at the foot of Police Coulee across from most of the glyphs, is a restored nineteenth-century North West Mounted Police post, one of a string of lonely outposts that guarded the border from horse thieves and whisky traders.

Writing-on-Stone

The park was originally set aside to protect the vision quest art on the cliffs above the Milk River, but the scenery and the wildlife are equally attractive. The rocks are sandstone, whittled by rain and wind; the river valley, with its shady willows and shrubs, provides home to many different species of birds, animals, snakes (yes, there are rattlesnakes here), and flowers.

St. Victor

The largest concentration of rock art in southern Saskatchewan is on a single cliff that rises 800 metres above the village of St. Victor. While most petroglyphs are carved into vertical faces, these 300 separate images were done on the horizontal, on the top of a flat-topped bluff on the northern edge of the Wood Mountain Plateau. On this single, multi-faceted surface, a strange world emerges, the world of the spirits, described in a very different art style (known as Plains Hoofprint Tradition) from that at Writing-on-Stone. Grinning faces, a few human and animal figures (including turtles), and a plethora of tracks—animal, bird, and human—are intermingled with human handprints and other shapes and symbols whose meanings have long since been lost. The most numerous of the footprints are those of the plains grizzly bear (there are eight) but there are also several bison tracks, some of them leading over the edge of the cliff. This suggests that the cliff itself might have been used as a buffalo jump, but archaeologists have found no evidence of this.

Drawings courtesy of Tim and Louise Jones, from the book Tracking Ancient Hunters.

David Munro photographs.

Considered very similar in style to rock art found in the American Midwest (the faces in particular), the St. Victor carvings could have been associated with hunting magic (the bison tracks) or shamanism: The grizzly featured prominently in early mythology, and turtles were symbols of longevity and fertility. Unlike the glyphs at Writing-on-Stone, there is little here that is familiar. Even the human faces and figures are strange. Only the handprints link us to the creators. Was the rock the site of vision quests? And were these strange designs created by the dreamers? And why was art inscribed only on this particular rock? There are other rock bluffs that would have provided just as good a canvas.

The rock is hard ravenscrag sandstone and no one is sure exactly when or how the carvings were done. (Were they drilled or carved or abraded?) Since some of the images were superimposed, it seems they were carved at different times, and perhaps by different tribes. Certainly, they all predate the coming of Europeans: There are no horses and no guns here.

For years, this special site was unprotected, and scores of people who came to picnic in the wooded coulee below walked and climbed all over it, hastening its deterioration. The sandstone is eroding: Chunks of rock, including some with petroglyphs on them, have already fallen. Today, the cliff is protected behind a wire fence, and visitors must walk on a protective boardwalk to see the glyphs. Like all great mysteries, they are hard to discern. Only the slanting light of morning or late evenings (or a floodlight in the dark) will reveal the carvings well enough for photography. And they also show up in the rain, the very rain that is helping to erase them. Nothing has been done to protect the carvings from the weather, and nothing will be. First Nations people have asked that the site be left alone to disappear naturally.

I met David Munro, of the Friends of St. Victor Petroglyphs, one summer evening. He had a key to open a gate in the wire fence, and we trod softly around the rock art to examine it at close hand. He pointed out several interesting glyphs, including his favourite: a man with his

right hand reaching up towards a circle, his left hand pointing to the earth and a large human footprint. What did it mean? He shrugged. Perhaps, he said, the man is taking knowledge from the world, the circle, and then he's handing it on. Later we sat and waited for the sun to go down and for the pictures on the rock to reveal themselves. They appeared on cue, as if by magic. St. Victor's is a splendid place, where one can feel the power of the spirit world.

The Wood Mountain Plateau itself is geologically interesting. It escaped the final scouring of the last Ice Age and holds fossilized remains of pre-glacial mammals, woolly rhinoceros, horses, and camels.

Travel Info

St. Victor's Petroglyphs Provincial Park lies south of Assiniboia and can be reached from Highway 2. The park is well signed, and a replica rock of the glyphs has been made for visitors to touch, photograph, and make rubbings. A group called The Friends of St. Victor Petroglyphs works to "preserve, protect, and promote" this fascinating site and raise money towards its upkeep. They have recorded all the petroglyphs, and photographs of them are on display in a small interpretive centre, along with some prehistoric pottery. There are also natural history exhibits, and a good little gift shop. In summer, the Friends' special events include night tours to the glyphs with solar-powered floodlights, wildflower walks, and butterfly catch-and-release studies.

The wooded coulee below the rock is a good area for wildlife and birds, while the short-grass prairie on top is bright with wildflowers in spring. It's a very special landscape. The sacred glyphs make it more so. For more info: contact the Friends: stvictor@sasktel.net; or Saskatchewan Parks: www.se.gov.sk.ca/saskparks/

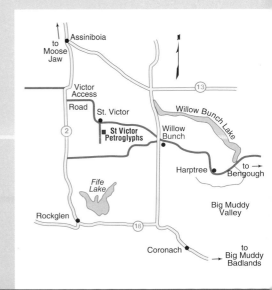

Rocky Mountain Sites

While by far the thickest clusters of known rock art sites lie on the grasslands, some have also been found on the eastern slopes of the Rockies. Pictographs painted in canyons here are different in style from those of the plains. It is thought that they belong to the tradition of Columbia Plateau Art,

Enigmatic men of Crossfield Coulee, Alberta.

mostly found in southeastern B.C. and Montana, and that they represent dreams and the acquisition of spiritual power obtained during a vision quest. Most of the pictographs are finger-painted in red ochre, coloured earth—easy to obtain from the badlands—pounded to a powder and mixed with some sort of grease. A few are black, made in charcoal-based paint.

Opposite: The beautiful figure of a man holding a hoop or a drum, in a canyon near Grassi Lakes, Alberta.

Grassi Lakes

In the Grassi Lakes area, also near Canmore, another beautiful canyon contains two rock art sites. One is a small cave or shelter, its entrance liberally smeared with red ochre, marking it as a spiritual place, where dreams could be born. In the centre of the canyon, a huge boulder displays, among others, a clear image of a man holding aloft a circular hoop or a drum; nearby is what could be a caribou. The canyon is steep and straight and wide, with a great view down into the valley of the Bow River.

This masked man lost most of his body because of rock shearing.
Photographs courtesy of Michael Klassen.

Pine Coulee

In Pine Coulee, west of Stavely, Alberta, all that is left of two very strange human figures are the head and shoulders, the rest of their bodies having weathered away. The face of one, shown in profile, has a very animal-like snout (perhaps he was wearing a mask?) and both hold what could be rattles, as if they were taking part in a ceremony. Experts have failed to find any rock art tradition that fits these strange figures: They are unlike any others in the lexicon.

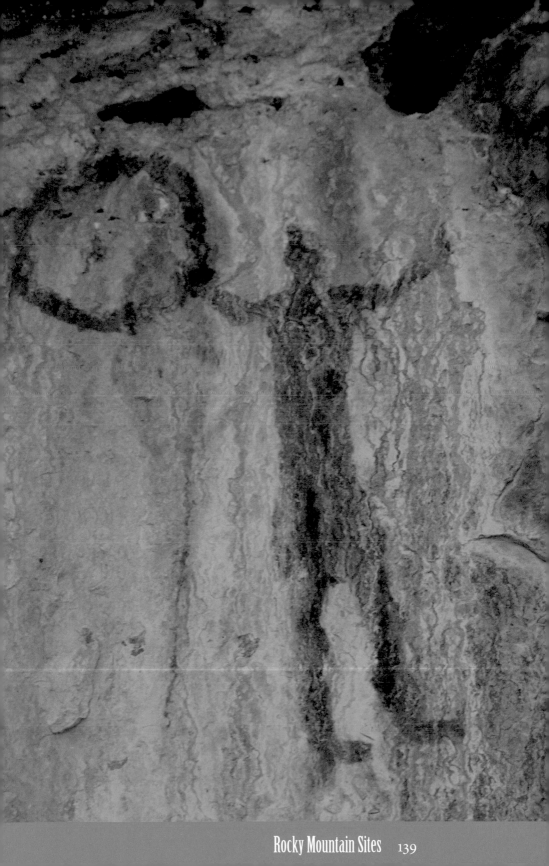

Zephyr Creek

A large number of Columbia Plateau pictographs have been found in the Zephyr Creek area southwest of Longview, in the foothills of Alberta. In a deep canyon near the confluence with Painted Creek, a small rock overhang on a south-facing dolomite spine once protected a group of six or eight red pictographs. But in 1975 some of the painted cliff collapsed. Today, there are only two figures, a man and an animal, to be seen at creek level. But high up along the crest of the rock rib are five more panels of human and animal figures, including two hunting scenes. In one, a buffalo stands victorious over the fallen figure of a hunter, watched by a dog or a coyote.

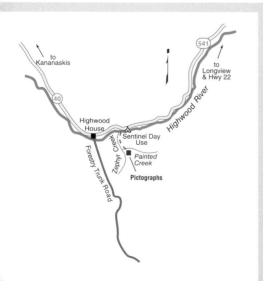

Travel Info

The Zephyr Creek pictographs are not easy to reach and involve a fairly difficult hike. Drive west from Longview (southwest of Calgary) on Highway 541 towards the mountains and park at the eastern edge of the Sentinel picnic area just before Highwood Junction. Wade across the Highwood River, then hike south, following Zephyr Creek to its confluence with Painted Creek, which enters from the east. The pictograph rock is about 500 m up Painted Creek on the north side of the canyon wall.

Grotto Canyon

The pictographs at Grotto Canyon have been described as the most exotic and unique in Alberta. The fact that they are very faint and filmed over with a thin, translucent mineral deposit, makes them seem doubly mysterious, literally veiled with the passage of time. The full details of these pictures were only recently revealed through modern technology: special polarized light photography and digital enhancement. One beautifully painted scene depicts a man with a long spear herding a group of elk. The man seems strange: His torso is tapered to a wasp-waist, and he has only one leg and big ears (possibly a headdress). In another scene, three of these one-legged beings stand side by side, their tapering bodies ending in tiny feet, or none at all. They all wear headdresses and carry ceremonial rattles—which look for all the world like giant ice cream cones. The art style has been classified as Fremont, which is mostly found in the southwestern U.S., about 600 kilometres south. Identical figures, a line of 10, are painted on the roof of a small cave in Carstairs Coulee, along with schematic renderings of a line of guns. This composition, in turn, is *almost exactly* the same as one painted on a buffalo robe in 1909 by Blackfoot elder Running Rabbit, who described his work as a historical record of the capture of many guns.

These one-footed figures are strange enough in Alberta, but the presence of a small, hunched-over figure apparently playing a flute, is stranger still. He has been recognized as Kokopelli, the hunchback trickster of the Anasazi (the ancestors of today's Hopi tribe), and he

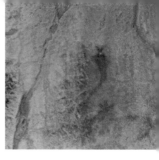

Filmed over by translucent mineral deposits, this ancient herder holds a staff and wears a headdress. Digital enhancement of the rock art enabled the drawings, below. Courtesy of the Heritage Community Foundation, Edmonton.

Travel Info

To make this magic journey follow Highway 1A east from Canmore, Alberta, for 10 km to the Grotto Mountain picnic area. Follow the signed Grotto Creek Trail through old growth forest for about 2 km into the canyon and look for the paintings on the west side at the base of a smooth cliff. They can be seen only if the light is just right. And your chances are better after rain. The cliffs in the canyon are used by rock-climbers; they keep clear of the painted sections.

Drawings of art in Grotto Canyon.
Courtesy of Michael Klassen.

Part of the Canyon wall.
Courtesy of the Heritage Community Foundation, Edmonton.

would be right at home on rock art panels in New Mexico or Utah, a thousand kilometres distant. The uncanny resemblance provides food for thought: Was there trade (in ideas as well as goods) that far south? Or did people from the south visit the canyon? Oral history suggests the latter. Hopi tradition tells of members of the Flute Clan who migrated north along the edge of the mountains until they came to a place covered with snow and ice. They couldn't live there and decided to move south again. Before they left, they made the mark of their Maahu, the flute-playing hunchback totem of their clan, to record where they had been.

These pictographs are beautiful and intriguing, well-matched to the splendour of their location, a narrow slot canyon carved by Grotto Creek on its chattering passage from the mountains to the plains. The canyon is narrow and twisting, a gloomy place, its cliffs overhung with dark spruce and pine trees. Where it reaches its narrowest point, a smooth, luminous limestone wall provides the pictograph canvas; beyond, the canyon appears to dead-end, but then twists and opens onto an alpine meadow. Perhaps the journey itself through the dark canyon into the light, a kind of birth, was part of the spiritual experience.

Crowsnest Cave

The power and beauty of the places where rock art is to be found make understandable the native notion of sacred landscape, inhabited by spirits both good and evil. Where the human and the spirit world appeared to converge—in a narrow canyon, in the split between two powerful rocks, in badland mazes or in caves (entrances to the underworld)—there was a belief that here the spirits could be summoned or appeased.

The three "wise men" of Grotto Canyon.

At Crowsnest Cave, in the Rockies that form the divide between British Columbia and Alberta, the infant Oldman River emerges from its rocky womb with an otherworldly rush. The sound of the water and the echoes are enough to raise a sense of unease in this place between darkness and light. Known to the Blackfoot as "Where the Oldman comes out of the Mountain," the cave was once smeared with ochre, and in 1881 geologist George Dawson reported the existence of painted glyphs. But vandalism has taken its toll—only a faint smear of ochre remains. It is still, nevertheless, a powerful place.

The Oldman River gushes from a cave in the Crowsnest Pass.
Michael Klassen photograph.

Erratics and Glyph Stones

Except for Writing-on-Stone and St. Victor's, rock art panels are rare on the Canadian grasslands. Why? There are hundreds of interesting cliffs along rivers and coulees that would have seemed suitable, at least from the practical aspect. Instead, small numbers of glyphs are found on single boulders, some of them enormous glacial erratics, others just small stones lying half-buried on prairie uplands. These seem to have been chosen because they were strange, oddly situated on the landscape, and often of a different colour or rock type. Perhaps they were believed to have come from an unearthly source and contained great spiritual power. Many of them, particularly the split ones, were also deliberately coated with blood red paint made from crushed rock and animal fat. Red ochre was a sign of the sacred, to early people throughout the world.

Drawing of the "weeping eye" face on an erratic boulder now at the Royal Saskatchewan Museum.

Split erratic in the Cabri Lake area near Eatonia, Saskatchewan.

The Erratics Train

The Okotoks erratic and thousands of others along the eastern foothills of the Rocky Mountains were carried south on the tongue of the most recent glacial advance. When the glaciers retreated, the rocks were left in a narrow, north-south band that stretches some 600 km into Montana. The erratics on this "train" have been in their present positions for between 12,000 and 18,000 years, dates obtained by a new method that measures cosmogenic chlorine 36 content (which tells how long rock has been out in the open air, bombarded by cosmic rays). Scientists have tracked the source of the rocks to a high mountain in Jasper National Park, and they have studied their distribution. The rock trail leads first east down the Athabasca River, then turns abruptly south as the ice front from the mountains (the Cordilleran) met the greater force of the Laurentide ice sheet coming from the northeast. The two ice fronts coalesced, preventing any kind of a passage for Ice Age humans until the ice began to retreat, around 11,000 to 11,500 years ago. The new dates add credence to the coastal migration theory of how humans first arrived in the New World.

The first people of the plains, who knew little about the movement of glacial ice, seem to have accepted the fact that these odd rocks must have come from somewhere else. They believed that, somehow, the spirits were involved.

Split Rock, Stavely

On the eastern edge of the Porcupine Hills, on the rim of a coulee that leads from Crocodile Lake, west of Stavely, Alberta, another glacial erratic stands 3.6 metres high and 4 metres wide. The rock is split to form an east-west passage, and a third section has slid across the passage to form a lintel. The sides of this cave-like passage have been liberally rubbed with red ochre. It has been suggested that the rhythmic movement involved in smearing paint repeatedly over rock was itself part of a religious ritual. On the ceiling of the "cave" are grooves, bird tracks, and several figures.

Okotoks

The largest glacial erratic in North America, this famous rock, 40 metres high and 18 metres wide, and estimated to weigh 16,500 tons, broke off a mountain in the Jasper area and was pushed by the ice to its present site near Okotoks, Alberta, about 10,000 years ago. To the Blackfoot, the split quartzite block has always been known simply as "the rock" or *okotoks*, a holy place where they leave offerings, usually of tobacco or sage. Much of its southern face is smeared with red ochre, and several small natural over-hangs protect abstract glyphs. Now an Alberta historic site, the rock is beside Highway 7 west of the town of Okotoks (named after it) and there are interpretive panels.

Napi's Rock

There is another split quartzite erratic (though much smaller) by the side of the road leading to Head-Smashed-In Buffalo Jump near Fort Macleod. The interpretive panel relates a Piikani legend that explains two things: how the rock was split and why the bat has a flat face. The story goes like this:

It was a hot day and Old Man Napi was tired. He threw his buffalo robe over a rock, saying, "Keep it, because you are poor and let me rest on you." And he rested there. When Napi walked on, it began to rain so Napi returned to the rock and took back his robe. The rock became angry and chased Napi furiously throughout the land. He ran for his life. Buffalo, deer, and antelope all tried to stop the rock, but the rock rolled right over them. Exhausted, Napi called on bats to help. They dove at the rock, and one hit it in the middle and broke it into two pieces. The fractured rock stopped running and Napi was saved. That is why all bats today have squashed-flat faces.

Standing Rock, Hazlet

West of Hazlet, Saskatchewan, another erratic, known as Standing Rock, was a critical landmark for pioneer settlers coming from the train at Gull Lake and travelling north to find their home-steads. Long before that, the rock was important to the buffalo people. A granite monolith, moved by ice from the Hudson Bay region and split into two chunks, it sits on a rise surrounded by several cairns and lines of boulders. The two pieces are far enough apart to permit easy passage, and one side of the slot is thickly spread with a deep red pigment. On top of this paint are two (maybe three) red handprints. If the people who made them wanted their handprints to stand out, why did they press them onto a surface already deeply stained with pigment of an almost identical colour? If you look carefully, you *can* see them, but only faintly. Perhaps the prints were not meant to be seen but to initiate transference of power from the spirit of the rocks. Handprints on granite are common in the lexicon of Precambrian Shield rock art, and versions also appear throughout the prairies.

Travel Info

To get to Hazlet drive north on Highway 7 from Gull Lake, then go west on Saskatchewan Highway 322. From Hazlet, the road continues west as Township Road 170. Standing Rock lies along the south side of this road; there is parking and an interpretive sign (which says nothing about the handprints).

Swift Current Petroglyph

It looks like an ordinary stone, similar to thousands of others you have probably walked by, but when you look at its location, on a rib of land that falls steeply to Swift Current Creek, Saskatchewan, and examine other stones in enigmatic clusters that lie nearby, you might want to stop and give it a second look. At midday, there is little to see, but near sunset, the angled light reveals a surface packed with strange incised designs.

David Green discovered the pictographs one evening as he was chasing cattle in the hills above the creek, within sight of his house. He had ridden and walked by the rock a hundred times before and had seen nothing. Only chance and slanting light had revealed its secrets. One summer evening, I sat by the stone and watched the designs materialize, as if by magic, as the sun went down. There appeared a long, straight line and several circles or bison tracks, possible turtles, a possible bear—as I looked at the stone from different angles I began to see many more figures. Only the little figure of a buffalo, deeply incised, remained constant. This site is interesting archaeologically because excavations around the rock unearthed two

The Swift Current Petroglyph is on private land, but luckily the owner provides B&B accommodation. Interested visitors can ask to see the magic stone, which lies on a hill across the creek. Call Swift Current Heritage B&B 306-773-6305, or look it up in the Saskatchewan accommodation guide.

curvaceous pictographs painted in black charcoal 20 centimetres below the soil. One was a clear depiction of some sort of animal with a beak and a long tail, the other, undecipherable. The pigment on these buried designs could be fairly firmly dated at around 1,200 years ago.

The glyphs on this stone gradually emerge in the slanting light of sunset, or in the beam of a flashlight, at night.

Mankota

It is likely that other rock art sites are yet to be found on the grasslands. I discovered one myself in a beautiful sandstone coulee on pastureland south of the community of Mankota in southern Saskatchewan. The coulee is well known to local people as a place to picnic, and the sandstone has been carved with scores of initials. Still, it is a beautiful landscape with eroded sandstone boulders pushing up from the hillside in a giant semicircle. A sharp hilltop nearby is crowned with a small cairn of slabs brilliant with red lichens. It is a spot to linger in, and I did. Poking about among the rocks, I found what seemed to me to be a prehistoric petroglyph, enigmatic lines that suggested a bird or a butterfly. I took a photograph and sent it off to be examined by experts. The site has yet to be authenticated.

Cabri Lake Petroglyph

In the Cabri Lake hills lies another petroglyph stone that reveals its treasures only in low light. Its situation is magnificent: at the end of a long, high ridge overlooking the folds of a curvaceous coulee. The ridgeback itself is covered with tipi rings, some of them enormous. The designs on this smooth, white stone are mostly linear, with a sinuous snake, a row of dots (like the cupules on a ribstone), and two eye-like circles (again, like the Herschel ribstone). This rock has not been studied.

Vision Quest Sites

Opposite page: Crownsnest Mountain, sacred to the Blackfoot.
Below: Results of a vision quest—the transference of power from a thunderbird, painted on a rock near Nanton, Alberta.
Courtesy of Michael Klassen.

The possibility of a parallel world of the spirit has intrigued mankind throughout the ages, and attempts to communicate with it, and perhaps to acquire some of its powers, have taken many forms. On the Canadian plains, these ventures took the form of a solitary vigil known as the vision quest.

Among the most elusive of all the man-made stone features on the Canadian grasslands, vision quest sites are simply places that were visited by young men seeking guidance from the spirit world. Many rock art sites were also used for vision quests (and many glyphs are believed to be the products of the visions), but there are others, less easy to identify. Small stone constructions, they are always isolated, usually in high places and within view of water. Most that have been identified in southern Alberta look towards one of three sacred places: Crownest Mountain, The Chief (across the U.S. border in Montana), and the Sweetgrass Hills, a hazy cluster of three sharp buttes (again in Montana) that dominate the southern horizon from such places as Writing-on-Stone and Manyberries.

A vision quest was not undertaken lightly. It entailed much instruction from tribal elders and ritual cleansing in a sweat lodge before the supplicant set forth. Once at the site, he fasted and

On the horizon, the beckoning blue of Montana's Sweetgrass Hills.

prayed in solitude and extreme exposure for three or four days. The visions (or hallucinations or dreams) of the supernatural that this sleep-deprived experience provoked helped him decide the course of his life. It was an out-of-body experience, a dream journey made through the landscape of the mind.

Because vision quest sites are remote, many have survived intact, and although it is difficult to prove their function, the power of these small stone structures is unmistakable. They, like medicine wheels and rock art sites, have a magnetic resonance, at least for some people. It has been suggested that all humans have, within their genetic makeup, an ability to detect changes in earth's magnetism (hence the ancient art of dowsing or witching for water), and that when we lived mostly out of doors we were aware of places on the planet where its magnetism is high. During prehistoric times, these places of power were chosen for medicine wheels, vision quests, and other sacred events. In the Old World, they became sites for ancient burials, stone megaliths, oracles, temples, and cathedrals. Today's industrialized society, alienated from the landscape, can no longer readily sense such subtle natural effects.

Mud Lake Vision Quest hill seen from the cliffs near the Head-Smashed-In drive lanes.

Obviously, not every cluster of rocks on a hilltop signifies a vision quest site

Chief Mountain

To the Blackfoot, Chief Mountain or Ninastako ("Stands Alone") is the home of the god Thunder who once stole a woman from the tribe and hid her in the mountain. The tribe called Raven down from his high abode on Crowsnest Mountain, and after a great battle involving lightning bolts and the freezing north wind, Raven made Thunder return the woman to her people. In another legend, Chief Mountain was the only land not submerged after the great flood, and it was from this high spot that Napi, the Creator, made the earth and all its inhabitants. The square summit crest of the Chief consists of a series of eroded rock spires and narrow cracks which produce a strange, hollow whistle—the music of the rocks—when the ever-fierce westerly winds blow through. The mountain must have been considered doubly holy when Thunder was speaking.

(also known as a dream bed). The construction is typically circular, oval, or horseshoe-shaped and about a metre across. The stones, often basalt or quartz, could be in a single layer, or built up to provide some shelter. Sites are usually accessible to both sunrise and sunset and focus on a special object, whether sacred mountain, river, or lake. They are more likely to be found in landscapes that are strange or spectacular, such as badlands.

Mud Lake

A striking vision quest site, one of the few that have been excavated, lies on a high knoll at the southwestern edge of the Porcupine Hills in southern Alberta, just a short distance from Head-Smashed-In Buffalo Jump. It is not known if the two sites are linked, but it seems probable. With an eagle's eye view east over Mud Lake to the flat prairies, and west to the Rockies, this is a heady place. There are at least two elements that fit the requirements for a dream bed: One is an oval long enough for a man to lie down in with a stone slab "pillow," and walls deep enough to

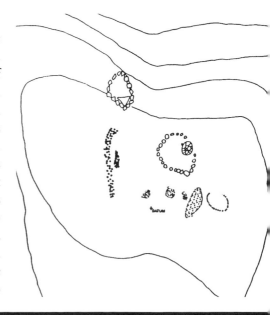

Cairn at the Mud Lake Vision Quest, with its view of plains and mountains.

provide some shelter; the other is a stone circle which may have been cannibalized in the recent past to build the adjacent stone cairn. Other configurations include a partly buried semicircle, open to the east, and a 15-metre-long ladder-like, linear arrangement of stones. (Detailed archaeological mapping proved that the latter actually spelled the name "Nelson Small Legs," a prominent leader of the American Indian movement who killed himself on the nearby Piikani Reserve to protest the plight of his people.)

Excavations at the site yielded only a few artifacts, including pieces of bone, seven projectile points, and a number of stone flakes. Interestingly, one of the stone points had been worked at the site: One of the flakes fitted perfectly back onto the sharpened blade. An excavation inside the large stone circle yielded only modern detritus: matches and two empty beer cans, perhaps left here when the cairn was built. The site is still used by the Piikani: Strips of coloured cloth and ribbons are frequently seen here.

Mapping in progress at one of the "dream beds."

Travel Info

Once or twice a year, specially guided hikes to the vision quest site, subject to landowner approval and guide availability, may be possible. Enquire at Head-Smashed-In Buffalo Jump near Fort Macleod. E-mail: info@head-smashed-in.com; phone: 403-553-2731; www.head-smashed-in.com

Manyberries

A cairn, just north of the Montana border in southeastern Alberta, marks another probable vision quest site. Originally believed to be a medicine wheel and burial site, the Manyberries Cairn sits on top of a mound once thought to be in the shape of a turtle. This was surrounded by a ring of large boulders, with stone circles and effigies

Graphic drawing of a vision quest experience.
Courtesy of Michael Klassen.

of a snake and a (possible) human figure nearby. Half the mound and the rock cairn were excavated in 1965 by a Glenbow Foundation crew who uncovered a burial pit with human remains and a variety of artifacts (including finger bones). The site was dated to 1,750 years ago.

However, re-examination of the site by John Dormaar indicated that though the mound was a natural feature, with stones added over time, a circular stone structure north of the mound was likely a vision quest site. The finger bones or phalanges found between the mound rocks could have been placed during such an experience. (Amputation, particularly of the top little finger joints, was a common practice, part of the self-sacrifice that helped to induce a vision.) The site is on a hill and looks south across the Milk River to the Sweetgrass Hills. The other stone formations nearby certainly implied to John a ceremonial place that would later have been attractive as a burial site. No historic-era artifacts were found in the burial pit, suggesting that the bones, those of an immature human, were buried prior to the European presence. The stone cairn, very close to the Montana border, may have been built in historic time, perhaps in 1899 by the North West Mounted Police (NWMP), who patrolled the area.

Milk River Canyon, east of Writing-on-Stone, one of the lonely places.

Travel Info

The Manyberries vision quest site lies in probably the most isolated part of southern Alberta, the Onefour substation, a research area of Agriculture Canada. It is difficult to access, but if you really want to go, you must call the Site Manager: 403-868-2364 for permission to enter the property.

Badlands

There are several other known vision quest sites in southeastern Alberta, most of them in the badlands of the Milk River Canyon and the Comrey Breaks. Perhaps the magnetism of these "other-worldly" places is particularly strong.

Badlands owe their existence to clouds of ash thrown into the atmosphere by the eruptions of ancient volcanoes. Millions of years ago, this volcanic ash settled over the shallow sea that once covered the prairies and mixed with its silt and sand. When the sea dried up, the sediments weathered into bentonite (a form of clay) and sandstone. This clay can absorb 10 times its volume in water, and after rainfall it becomes very slippery, far too slick for driving—or even walking. Once the clay has absorbed all it can, it forms an impermeable layer that prevents rain from soaking into the soil beneath. More rainfall simply runs down the hills, causing rapid erosion and sculpting the contorted forms that make badlands so fascinating. Wind erosion adds the finishing touches. The Blackfoot and Cree peoples believed that hoodoos were petrified giants, who, if not treated with respect, would hurl rocks down onto intruders who came into their territory at night.

Dinosaur Park

On a bluff overlooking the eerie badlands of the Red Deer River, rusty red lichens colour a nest of stone slabs that readily suggests a "dream bed." To lie here, in deep thirst, in the scorch of a dryland summer, would indeed provoke visions. What a temptation the cool river water would have been. This ancient site and several others are inside the park's natural area, out of bounds to visitors. Dinosaur Provincial Park is near Brooks, Alberta, and is best known for its paleontology sites.

John Dormaar photo.

John Dormaar photo.

Grasslands

On a surpringly sharp little knob of a hill enfolded within voluptuous grasslands, a circle of colourful rocks, deeply embedded and covered with lichens, provided a dream bed for spirit searchers in Grasslands National Park, Saskatchewan.

Bear Hills

North of the little town of Harris, in Saskatchewan, the hill country has been gently treated by the passing years, its grassy swales and hummocks mostly still untouched grazing land. I was introduced to the area by retired farmer and photographer George Tosh, accompanied by Betty McFarlane, who runs the Harris Museum, and Albert Longworth, whose cattle range the hills. We drove in convoy into the area, then took off on foot through the hills. Here I was shown several very interesting archaeological sites, including a "turtle rock," at least two vision quest sites, a large buffalo rubbing stone, rock cairns and lines, and a constellation of stone rings of many sizes.

In the world of the buffalo hunters, effigies didn't have to be created on the land if they were already there. The Turtle Rock, a huge limestone erratic glowing with rusty lichen, sits on a south-facing hillside. From certain angles, a very realistic turtle appears to crouch on the top, its head in the air. The rock is thought to be the centrepiece of a ceremonial site that includes several large, deeply embedded stone circles. Constructed turtle effigies are found elsewhere in Saskatchewan. Perhaps the natural formation on top of this rock is part of this turtle tradition.

This huge stone circle is one of the largest in the "Valley of the Nine Rings" in the Bear Hills (see aerial photograph page 12).
George Tosh photograph.

Also in the Bear Hills are two stone-circle vision quest sites, both in high and scenic locations. They have been disturbed but their essential characteristics remain: hollows in the earth bordered with rocks for shelter. In one, bushes have grown up, sprung from seeds carried by birds or the wind to a sacred spot no longer visited for visions. It provides wide-reaching views in all directions and overlooks alkali lakes to the west. (A view of water is one of the apparent requirements for a vision quest site.) In a valley, more than 200 metres directly below (known to local amateur archaeologists as "The Valley of the Nine Rings"), lies a cluster of nine stone circles, and on slightly higher ground beyond there are another four very large ones, one of which is a regular spring dancing ground—a lek for sharp-tailed grouse. The second vision quest site is an oval, oriented north-south, a shallow depression lined and edged with stones. Turtle Rock can be clearly seen to the southwest.

Travel Info

To visit the Bear Hills sites near Harris, SK, contact the Eagle Creek Historical Society at 306-237-9161.

Mountain fireweed in the Kananaskis.

Mountain Sites

Those who spend time in the mountains can attest to the sweet feeling of success attained on reaching a summit—and then, looking down, of humility, as one considers the insignificance of a single human compared to the awe-inspiring spread of the sky and the earth below. Are these feelings part of the inspiration of high peaks?

The eastern foothills of the Rockies are known to house several very lofty vision quest sites, and Crowsnest Pass and Waterton Park also seem to have been attractive, providing potential views of two "sacred" mountains, the Chief and Crowsnest. On a high mountain saddle in the Pincher Creek area, a six-metre circular dream bed, with a small fireplace in front, faces Crowsnest Mountain. At Fording River Pass, a vision quest site in the shape of a single enormous boulder, with a depression in one corner for seating, lies beside an old native trail through the mountains. Another site also perches on a ridge, fairly close to the Zephyr Creek pictographs at the south end of the Highwood Range.

None of these mountain sites is protected, apart from the natural safeguard that isolation and difficult access provide. If you're hiking in the hills and come across rocks that could be a vision quest or other native structure, treat the site with respect. The removal of even one stone could destroy its validity.

Chief Mountain, Montana, across fields of Alberta grain.

Eagle Traps

Some of the small, circular, stone-lined pits found on high ground throughout the prairies are thought to have been used to trap eagles. Evidence for this use by several Plains tribes has been well-documented. Eagle feathers were and still are important sacred items: They are used for amulets and adornment, particularly for headdresses. Difficult to obtain, in pre-European days they were valuable items of trade: In the world of the Hidatsa, 12 eagle feathers would trade for a horse. Before the advent of guns, trapping these giant birds for their feathers entailed rituals akin to those of the vision quest, followed by a feat of great daring. On a high hill, a stone pit was made deep enough for a man to crouch inside, and brush was piled over the top. A decoy, perhaps a live rabbit or a piece of meat, was tied to the brush and the long vigil began. When an eagle finally landed to take the bait, his feet were grabbed from below by the man in the pit and the bird was pinioned—no easy matter: An eagle has tearing talons and a huge wingspan. Sometimes the tail feathers were plucked and the bird released, but more often the bird was kept captive for a while or killed and all its feathers used. A whole eagle's wing became a fan, an item still used today by dancers at a powwow.

This Siksika dance bustle uses an eagle's head as well as its feathers.

Deep stone pit in the Cabri Lake Hills: Is it an eagle trap or a signal fire pit?
George Tosh photograph.

An eagle wing fan, used in some traditional dances.

Other Prehistoric Places

Opposite: This narrow passage, cut through the Rockies by the Oldman River, is known as the Livingstone Gap.

Old Man's Bowling Green

No one with an interest in ancient historical places should miss a visit to the Old Man's Bowling Green, a site where everything is left to the imagination. Its intriguing alignments of stones have been scoured away by river floods, and the site is known in detail only through written accounts. Peter Fidler, the first Hudson's Bay Company explorer to visit Alberta's southern foothills, described it well, and left a drawing. More than 100 years later, geologist George Dawson also made mention of it in one of his reports. It was known to early ranchers, and as late as 1965 an archaeologist reported seeing cairns on the site; some excavations took place, but only after the "evidence" had gone. Today, like so much of the First People's history, it lies only in the mind.

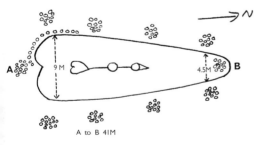

It was the end of December in 1792 when Fidler and a group of Piikani travelled along the Oldman River and through the dramatic limestone canyon known today as the Livingstone Gap. Fidler stopped to look at an unusual arrangement of stones laid out on a meadow beside the river, just east of the confluence with Racehorse Creek. On New Year's Eve, he made a sketch and wrote this description in his journal:

"It is a place where Indians formerly assembled here to play at a particular Game by rolling a small hoop of 4 inches diameter and darting an Arrow out of the hand after it & those that put the arrow through the hoop while rolling along is reckoned to have gamed. This is on a fine

level grass plain, very little bigger than the enclosed space. One side is within 10 yards of the river & the direction of this curiosity is directly one North & south. All those peaces that compose the outer and inner parts are small stones set close together about the bigness of a person's fist above the ground & they are so close set and so neatly put together that it appears one entire ledge of stones."

Fidler then gave the Piikani account of the place, an explanation that he thought was "surprising and ridiculous": "They say that a white man came from the south many ages ago and built this for the Indians to play at, that is different nations whom he wished to meet here annually & bury all anemosities betwixt the different tribes by assembling here and playing together. They also say that this person made the Buffalo, on purpose for the Indians. They described him as a very old white headed man …"

A hoop-and-arrow game was played in historic time by many different tribes of North America, including the Mandan villagers from the south. Was this old man one of the Cluny immigrants? Or were the Piikani referring to Napi, their "Old Man," the maker of buffalo and all other things on Earth?

A hoop-and-arrow game, similar to that described by Fidler, was played in historic time by the Cree and other tribes.

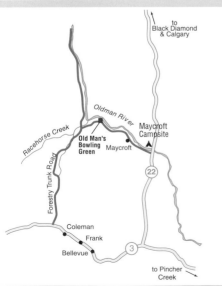

Travel Info

The site of the Old Man's Bowling Green beside the Oldman River can easily be found: It lies on the south bank less than a kilometre below the confluence with Racehorse Creek. There is a level meadow here and there are plenty of fist-sized stones. Take Fidler's plan and lay them all out, in your head. See the place as it used to be. Alberta Highway 22 crosses the Oldman River beside the small campsite of Maycroft. Take the road leading west along the river and through the Oldman Gap. Park just before you reach the Forestry Trunk Road and find the meadow, on a north-south section of the river that corresponds with Fidler's description. The river is loud and lovely; in summer the canyon is bright with fireweed.

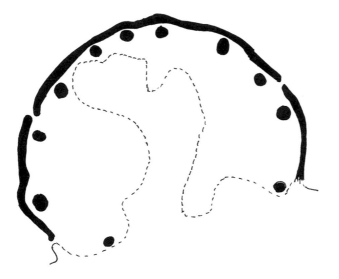

Plan of the Cluny village showing supposed house pits and ditch.

Cluny Earth Lodge Village

At most of the prehistoric sites on the Canadian grasslands stone provides the structure for investigations of the past. But at one intriguing place in southern Alberta, no stone is involved—simply post holes and excavations in the earth. Occupied only briefly by strangers, it is perhaps the most puzzling of the ancient sites on the grasslands.

The site lies on Siksika reserve lands east of Calgary, but the Siksika know that it does not belong to their forefathers. On the lip of a long-abandoned river cutbank lies an ancient village, once fortified by a semicircular ditch and a log palisade. It is unlike the tipi villages of the plains; circular depressions in the ground point to a different form of habitation—the earth lodges common to the Mandan and Hidatsa who live farther to the southeast. These people were not primarily hunters, but farmers, who grew corn, squash, and beans. Why did these agriculturalists trek north, build a fortified village, occupy it only briefly, and then abandon it? The mystery may never be completely solved.

The village site, which lies south of Cluny, close to Blackfoot Crossing, traditionally the most important ford on the Bow River, has been well documented. The North West Mounted

Aerial view of the Cluny Earth Lodge site.
Courtesy of Glenbow Archives
B132-A-203.

Mandan earth lodges in North Dakota were bigger than the "housepits" excavated at Cluny, below. Glenbow Archives C116-135.

Police (NWMP) in 1875 reported an old encampment that went "farther back than the Indians have any record." The Marquis of Lorne, out exploring the colonies in 1881, described "an old earthwork with a circular fosse." And the same year, geologist George Dawson left a good account of a "fortified camp surrounded by a shallow trench of semi-circular outline, 400 feet in greatest diameter and with 10 well-defined hollows along its inner margin." In 1911, artist Edmund Morris described, in the *Canadian Magazine*, "an ancient fort made by the Crow Indians where they took their last stand against the Blackfoot." He dug inside the fortifications and uncovered hearth sites, pottery, stone tools, and bones. He drew the village in the shape of a horseshoe, with 10 pits like keyholes.

Archaeologist Richard Forbis excavated at the Cluny site in 1960, helped by members of the Siksika Nation. He found the ditch to be 2.5 metres wide and one metre deep, broken in several places for entrances. Five to six metres inside the ditch there had been a palisade of cottonwood logs embedded in a trench, and this was supported by large vertical posts. (Post holes and even some of the wood remained.) And there were 11 circular pits. The fortifications alone represented a great deal of hard labour with wood

and bone tools over many months; when dry, the prairie soil is hard to break, even with a pick and shovel.

But were the 11 circular pits the remains of houses? Only four metres wide, far smaller than a typical Mandan earth lodge, they lay outside, not inside the defensive palisade, which seems strange enough. There was also no evidence of roof supports or of central hearths. Forbis could only suppose that they were *not* houses at all, but part of the fortifications and that perhaps the villagers lived in tipis inside the palisade.

The village was definitely pre-contact (excavations uncovered no historical items). A few horse bones were excavated so Forbis knew the site had to be later than AD 1725 (when the first Spanish horses arrived on the plains). Testing of wood post remnants proved him right: Carbon 14 dates came in at around 1740. Artifacts recovered included clay discs (perhaps used for gaming), pieces of pottery, stone tools and projectile points, shell discs, bone beads, two copper knives, and several mortars and pestles, all indications of a culture different from that of the buffalo hunters. The mortars and pestles suggested a reliance on grains. But the villagers didn't seem to have been farmers: No digging implements were found. (Early agriculturalists made hoes from bison scapula and rakes with antler tines.) Who were these people?

Perhaps the greatest mystery of all was this: Why did the strangers who spent so much time and energy building a fortified village abandon it so soon? Forbis calculated, from the number of artifacts, that the village had been

A hoe made from bison scapula and a rake from antler tines, typical of the tools the Cluny people might have used, if they had come to Alberta from the Missouri Villages.

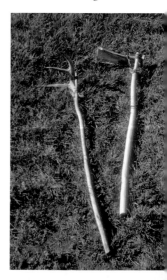

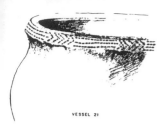

VESSEL 21

VESSEL 1

VESSEL 11

Reconstructions of pots from sherds found at Cluny—new designs for Alberta.

inhabited for no more than a couple of months, then abandoned. There were no signs of disaster, no bones of battle, no scorching from fire, no mass burials from disease epidemics. Why and where did they go?

Fortunately, they did not vanish without a trace. They left behind a very distinctive form of pottery, one that prehistoric Alberta had not seen before. From the more than 2,000 pottery sherds found in the village, some could be pieced together enough to show they had come from globular jars 17 or 18 centimetres in diameter. The pots had collared rims and were decorated with grooved paddle impressions and stamped linear designs, mostly chevrons and triangles. These pots were similar but tantalizingly different from those made along the Middle Missouri in the eighteenth-century. This unique pottery shows up in other sites in Alberta, making what one archaeologist called "a sudden and dramatic entrance to Alberta between 1720 and 1750"—coincidental with the presence of Cluny visitors. Pottery was traditionally a woman's task. Did some of the Cluny women marry into other tribes, taking with them their traditional pottery designs? Or did they trade the pottery for other goods, perhaps meat from the buffalo hunters?

Siksika oral history reaches back a long time. Questioned in 1960, a history keeper called One Gun, born in 1883 (he was the first to lead archaeologists to the site), recounted how the people who made the fortified village were a splinter group from a large tribe in the U.S. They were friendly with the Siksika. They came from the south, stayed for one winter, and returned to the south, taking two Siksika with them. They had dogs but no horses (yet horse bones were found on the site). Much of this substantiates the archaeologists' findings.

Cluny Earth Lodge Village has been declared a national historic site, though no further excavations have been done and many of the mysteries have yet to be explained. Lying on Siksika land, the site is close to two of the most important historic places of the plains people, the ford (known as Blackfoot Crossing) across the Bow River and the gravesite of the great Chief Crowfoot. While the mysterious village is not of Siksika origin, they protect it well.

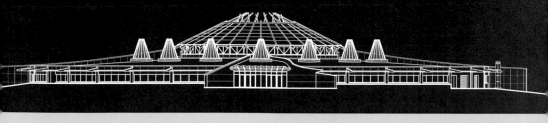

Blackfoot Crossing

The Siksika's new Blackfoot Crossing Interpretive Centre, an imaginative piece of architecture in the shape of a tipi cover, laid flat, is built into the hillside above the river flats, within view of the enigmatic earth lodge village and other historic sites. Architect Ron Goodfellow's design wove together many facets of Siksika architecture—the tipi, the sundance circle, the buffalo women's lodge, and the dance arbor—to commemorate the rich traditions of the First Nations. Like a traditional tipi, the centre's entrance faces east, towards the rising sun. The tops of seven tipis pierce the roof, and four of them continue down to the main floor to delineate circular galleries where the lifeways of the Siksika and other members of the Blackfoot Nation will be explained. Below the bluffs, interpretations will continue at the Earth Lodge Village and there will be walks and tours to other Siksika sites, including Chief Crowfoot's Grave, a medicine wheel, an antelope trap, a buffalo rubbing stone, a battlefield, and even the remains of a whisky trader's fort. The centre will be open to the public in 2006.

Members of the Mandan First Nations of North Dakota have been invited to examine the earth lodge village site, the pottery, and other relics to see if they can shed light on the mysterious visitors. What they say may well determine the village's fate: to be left as it is, bush-filled depressions on the river terrace, or to be re-excavated, with the new tools and techniques that modern archaeology now has. For information on the Blackfoot Crossing Historical Interpretive Centre contact the Siksika Band Office: 403-264-7250. The centre lies south of Cluny beside Secondary Road 842, just before you cross the Bow River.

A young dancer at the Siksika Fair.

Wanuskewin

Along the west bank of the South Saskatchewan River north of Saskatoon, is a national historic site called Wanuskewin. This is an unusual bicultural park, one that seeks to interpret not only contemporary archaeology, but also pre-contact history and the culture of native Canadians. Its name is Cree for "seeking peace of mind," and all of Saskatchewan's five First Nations peoples took part in its planning. Band members also contribute with interpretation, demonstrate native crafts, dancing, and drumming and supply many of the staff. Because to them it is a sacred place, here, away from the public gaze, they still hold traditional ceremonies.

The site encompasses 116 hectares of prairie and the deep, wooded valley of Opimihaw Creek, where there is evidence of continued episodes of occupation over the past 8,000 years. It is a place unusually rich in First Nations sites; 19 have been found here, including bison kills (a jump as well as a pound), tipi rings, and a 1,500-year-old medicine wheel. Interconnecting trails describe four different discovery routes where the native camps and other sites, including active archaeological digs, are well signed and explained.

Visitors to Wanuskewin begin by following bison tracks in the cement walkway along ancient drive lanes, past statues of charging buffalo, into the interpretive centre, its roof like the peaks of a tipi, divided into four segments. (Four is the sacred number of the Plains First People, representing the cardinal directions, the seasons, and the earth elements.) The different areas of the building radiate from a central buffalo pound, complete with two life-sized bison. There's an interior storytelling circle, an interpretive museum, laboratory, and gift shop, and outside, an amphitheatre where aboriginal dancing and

drumming take place. In the restaurant, buffalo stew, bannock, wild rice, and Saskatoon pie are on the menu. The native presence is everywhere.

Wanuskewin is a good place to end this journey of discovery. Visitors will come away convinced that the heritage of the First Nations people is not confined to museums and archaeological reports, but alive and well, part of the grand mosaic of Canadian society. At places like Writing-on-Stone, Head-Smashed-In, St. Victor's, Herschel, and the Majorville Cairn, the past can come vividly alive.

Tipis at Wanuskewin. They are available for campers who sign up for a cultural experience. www.wanuskewin.com

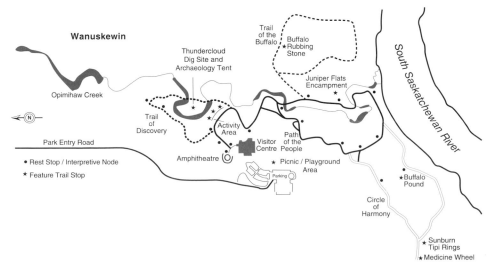

Wanuskewin

Opimihaw Creek

Thundercloud Dig Site and Archaeology Tent

Trail of the Buffalo

Buffalo Rubbing Stone

Juniper Flats Encampment

South Saskatchewan River

Trail of Discovery

Activity Area

Path of the People

Visitor Centre

Amphitheatre

Parking

Picnic / Playground Area

Circle of Harmony

Buffalo Pound

Park Entry Road

• Rest Stop / Interpretive Node

★ Feature Trail Stop

Sunburn Tipi Rings

Medicine Wheel

Suggested Reading

Barry, P.S. *Mystical Themes in Milk River Rock Art.* Edmonton: University of Alberta Press, 1991.

Berry, Susan and Jack Brink. *Aboriginal Cultures in Alberta: Five Hundred Generations.* Edmonton: Provincial Museum of Alberta, March 2005.

Blackfoot Gallery Committee, Glenbow Museum. *Nitsitapiisinni: The Story of the Blackfoot People.* Toronto: Key Porter Books, 2001.

Brace, Ian G. *Boulder Monuments of Saskatchewan.* Saskatoon: Saskatchewan Archaeological Society, 2005.

Brink, Jack and John Dormaar, eds. *Archaeology in Alberta: A View from the New Millennium.* Medicine Hat: Archaeological Society of Alberta, 2003.

Bryan, Liz. *The Buffalo People: Precontact Archaeology on the Canadian Plains.* Surrey: Heritage House, 2005.

Dempsey, Hugh A. *Indian Tribes of Alberta.* Calgary: Glenbow Museum, 1978.

Devereux, Paul. *Stone Age Soundtracks: The Acoustic Archaeology of Ancient Sites.* London: Vega Books, 2001.

Dewar, Elaine. *Bones: Discovering the First Americans.* Toronto: Vintage Canada, 2001.

Dormaar, J. and R.L. Barsh. *The Prairie Landscape: Perceptions of Reality.* Prairie Conservation Forum, Paper #3, 1999.

Epp, Henry T. *Long Ago Today: The Story of Saskatchewan's First Peoples.* Saskatoon: Saskatchewan Archaeological Society, 1991.

Epp, Henry, T. and Ian Dyck, eds. *Tracking Ancient Hunters: Prehistoric Archaeology in Saskatchewan.* Regina: Saskatchewan Archaeological Society, 1983.

Forbis, Richard. *Cluny: An Ancient Fortified Village in Alberta*. Calgary: University of Calgary. Dept. of Archaeology, Occasional Paper #4, 1977.

Friends of Grasslands, Inc. Staff. *Grasslands National Park Field Guide*. Val Marie, Saskatchewan: Prairie Wind & Silver Sage, Friends of Grasslands, Inc., 2000.

Helgason, Gail. *The First Albertans: An Archaeological Search*. Edmonton: Lone Pine, 1987.

Huck, Barbara and Doug Whiteway. *In Search of Ancient Alberta: Seeking the Spirit of the Land*. Winnipeg: Heartland Publications, 1998.

Keyser, James D. and Michael A. Klassen. *Plains Indian Rock Art*. Vancouver: UBC Press/University of Washington Press, Seattle, 2001.

Kooyman, Brian and Jane Kelly, eds. *Archaeology on the Edge*. Calgary: University of Calgary Press, 2004.

Koppel, Tom. *Lost World: Rewriting Prehistory—How New Science is Tracing America's Ice Age Mariners*. New York: Atria Books, 2003.

McGhee, Robert. *Ancient Canada*. Ottawa: Canadian Museum of Civilization, 1989.

Pard, Bernadette. *The Peigan: A Nation in Transition*. Edmonton: Plains Publishing Inc., 1986.

Time-Life Books Staff. *The Buffalo Hunters*. Virginia: Alexandria, Time Life Books, 1993.

Index of Sites